ESSENTIAL
GUIDE TO YOUR
401(k) PLAN

VIRGINIA B. MORRIS
KENNETH M. MORRIS

LIGHTBULB
PRESS ®

LIGHTBULB PRESS
Project Team

Design Director Dave Wilder
Editors Paul Benzon, Megan Costa, Karen W. Lichtenberg
Design Kara W. Hatch
Design Assistant Katharina Szutkowski
Production and Illustration Antonina Colbert, Holly Duthie, Christopher Engel, Cadence Giersbach, Gary Lingard, James R. Lowenhaupt, Terry Marks, Mike Mulhern, Fanny Neira, Noah L. Rodriguez, Thomas F. Trojan, Edie Winograde

Sales and Marketing Germaine Ma, Karen Meldrom, Karen Cantor

SPECIAL THANKS
Yaqub Ahmed, Regional Managing Director, Trustar Retirement (a trade name of Trust Consultants), Iris Bernstein, Holly Bendriham, Dianne Hatch, Eric Simons, David Spanierd, David L. Wray

LIGHTBULB
PRESS ®

*T*wenty years ago almost no one had heard of 401(k) plans. Today more than 40 million people have money invested in these retirement savings accounts. Millions of other working Americans participate in similar plans, such as 403(b), 457, and thrift savings plans.

Thanks to the tax-deferred nature of 401(k)s—no tax is due on earnings until the money is withdrawn—plan participants have a prime opportunity to accumulate wealth for long-term financial security. And for a growing number of people, the 401(k) account is becoming their single most valuable asset, creating a new group of 401(k) millionaires.

Despite the popularity of 401(k)s—some 340,000 companies currently offer them—and the combined value of the accounts (estimated at $1.7 trillion), it's surprising how many people don't know the basics about their plans, such as how much they can contribute each year, or the potential penalties for certain withdrawals. Many others feel they don't have enough information to make informed investment decisions. There's even greater confusion about more complicated issues—for example, what happens to 401(k) accounts when participants change jobs, or how much money they must take as an annual distribution when they retire.

We've created this guide to answer these and other essential questions about 401(k)s. The guide explains why you should enroll in your employer's plan, what investments to look for, and how to manage your 401(k) portfolio. It also tells you what you need to know about rolling over 401(k) assets to a new employer's plan or individual retirement account (IRA), what to consider in choosing a beneficiary, and special 401(k) features that can help you in a pinch.

As you read the guide, you should be aware that the laws governing 401(k)s have changed frequently in the past, and are likely to do so again in the future. So it's important to keep up-to-date by reading the materials provided by your employer, or visiting our website at www.lightbulbpress.com for regular updates.

In Lightbulb's signature style, we have used clear language and lively graphics to illustrate crucial concepts and provide you with practical, helpful information. Whether you're already participating in a plan or thinking about joining one, we hope that you find this guide a useful companion in making important 401(k) decisions and getting the most from your plan.

Virginia B. Morris   Kenneth M. Morris

ESSENTIAL GUIDE TO YOUR 401(k) PLAN

OVERVIEW

401(K) PLAN BASICS

INVESTING IN YOUR 401(K)

CONTENTS

MANAGING YOUR 401(K)

SPECIAL 401(K) FEATURES

401(K) WITHDRAWALS

401(K) WITHDRAWALS STRATEGIES

A Short History of Retirement

Retirement income isn't a new idea, but ideas about it have changed over the years.

Before the end of the 19th century, most employers didn't think much about how people who grew too old to work could afford to live. After all, in 1900, a man's life expectancy was 47, and men were the majority of the workforce.

But social and economic forces working together gradually helped change attitudes toward how people were paid while they worked and after they retired. Some employers offered the promise of a pension rather than pay higher wages. Others recognized their responsibility to people who spent entire careers on the job. And the federal government began to support retiring civilian workers to parallel the support it had long provided to disabled war veterans.

The creation of Social Security in the wake of the depression that followed the stock market crash of 1929 was probably the single most important piece of legislation in US pension history. It recognized the government's responsibility to make financial provisions for the aging population. And it set the stage for the expansion of private pensions as well.

PENSION RIGHTS

The newly independent colonies institute modest pensions for disabled Revolutionary War soldiers and their dependents, a practice that has continued for veterans of all other US wars. (One long-lived son of a Revolutionary soldier was still collecting in 1901.)

The Social Security Act is signed into law, providing retirement income to participating civilian workers and their families.

1630   1776   1875   1935

Massachusetts colonists pay the first recorded pensions in North America to soldiers injured in fighting with Native Americans.

The American Express Company, a railroad corporation, introduces the first private pension plan. By 1929, there are 397 pension plans in operation.

A LONG   HISTORY

Though savings for retirement by contributing pretax salary to a 401(k) plan has a relatively short history—dating back only to 1981—the Revenue Acts of 1921, 1926, and 1928 lay the groundwork for this arrangement. The laws exempt investment earnings from trusts from current taxation, and permit tax-deductible employer contributions for amounts larger than what is currently due to the employee.

PRIVATE PENSIONS

Like Social Security, private pensions have contributed to a more secure retirement for millions of workers. While a few hundred pension plans predate the 1940s, most of the pension plans operating in the early 21st century have been created since World War II.

That was a turning point for retirement benefits, partly because employers competing for workers were prevented from offering higher salaries by the rigid wage and price controls the government enacted to control inflation. But since promising future income was legal, offering pensions was one way large corporations could attract workers.

After the war, in the face of a booming economy and chronic labor shortages, labor unions were able to negotiate pension rights for their members. At the same time, pension promises became important recruiting tools as corporations competed for white collar and professional employees. By the 1960s, most employees who weren't in line for some type of retirement income worked for small companies or in jobs that had not been unionized.

The Employee Retirement Income Security Act (ERISA) sets funding,

reporting, disclosure, and operating standards for pension plan administrators and requires uniform vesting rights for plan participants. The Act introduces IRAs, makes it easier for the self-employed to establish pension plans, and makes stock ownership plans part of the tax code. It also makes the plan sponsor and other officials legally responsible for operating plans for the benefit of employees and their beneficiaries.

The IRS approves the use of Section 401(k) to allow employees to reduce their taxable salaries by making pretax contributions to an employer sponsored plan. The effect is to shift responsibility for providing retirement income to employees participating in plans offered by employers.

401(k)

1958   1974   1978   1981   NOW

Welfare and Pension Plan Disclosure Act requires pension plans to provide employees with enough information so they can protect themselves from fiduciary abuses. In 1962, amendments to the act give the federal government responsibility for limiting abuses.

The Revenue Act includes Section 401(k), which permits qualified deferred compensation plans. These plans allow employees to postpone income tax on pay they agree to collect at a later date, typically when they retire.

SOCIAL SECURITY

When Social Security was enacted in 1935, it was a controversial program designed to cope with widespread unemployment and poverty among the elderly, many of whom were in dire circumstances. Today, more than 90% of US workers and their families participate in the program, paying a percentage of their wages for future coverage, or collecting a monthly payment based on their past contributions.

More than 95% of the households with someone over 65 get benefits. In fact, without Social Security income, more than half of the elderly population would be classified as poor by government standards. But because of those benefits, fewer than 10% are in that situation.

A shrinking working population coupled with an increasing retiree population poses some threat to Social Security's long-term viability. In 1950, there were 16 contributors for every beneficiary. In 2001, there are only three people contributing for every person drawing benefits. But Social Security in some form will continue to be a cornerstone of retirement income well into the 21st century.

So What's the Plan?

There are two kinds of retirement plans: some focus on benefits and others focus on contributions.

If you're in a defined benefit plan, the benefit is that you'll get a pension, or fixed retirement income, from your employer. If you're in a defined contribution plan, the contribution is defined, which means money is contributed in your name to a retirement plan. The assets you've accumulated when you retire are based on how much is put into the plan, how it is invested, and its investment performance.

WHAT YOU GET

With a traditional **defined benefit plan**, the size of your pension generally depends on how much you're earning at the end of your career and on the number of years you've worked for your employer. The more you make and the longer you've been there, the more you're likely to get.

With a newer, and sometimes controversial, defined benefit plan called a **cash balance plan**, time on the job weighs more heavily than final salary in determining your retirement income.

With a **defined contribution plan**, such as a profit sharing or stock bonus plan, the more that's contributed in your name over a period of time, the larger your investmentment account has the potential to grow.

But both cash balance plans and defined contribution plans are usually **portable**, which means that when you change jobs you can take the benefit with you or roll it into an IRA so you can continue to build on the assets that you have accumulated.

WHO CONTRIBUTES, WHO DECIDES

When employers offer a defined benefit plan, they create and fund a corporate pension account, and invest the fund's assets to meet their obligation to you and other retired workers.

Employers who offer a defined contribution plan can contribute to your account themselves, allow you to defer part of your salary into the plan, or both. In some defined contribution plans, your employer determines how the plan assets are invested. More frequently, you select investments from a menu of choices. When that's the case, your plan is **self-directed**, and the retirement income you get will be determined by the investments

you make. Whether you see this responsibility as an opportunity or a burden depends largely on the quality of your investment choices, and how comfortable you are in deciding among them.

IT'S A PLAN?

A 401(k) plan isn't actually a retirement plan at all. It's a section of the Internal Revenue Code that lets you contribute pre-tax salary to a profit sharing or stock bonus plan. But neither that technicality—nor its unimaginative name—has stood in the way of the phrase *401(k) plan* being widely used to describe this popular way of saving for retirement.

DO YOU KNOW THE CODA?

In retirement terms, a CODA is a beginning, not an ending, as it is in a musical composition. It's short for cash or deferred arrangement, which is the foundation for 401(k) plans. It gives you, as an employee, the right to decide whether to take a payment in cash or to defer it. The right to choose must be a real one. Your employer can't make your eligibility for other benefits contingent upon your agreement to defer compensation.

Defined Benefit

Defined Contribution

TO DO

CAUTION

WHEN RESULTS DON'T MEASURE UP

If you're responsible for investing your retirement plan assets, it helps to know where things can go wrong. If you know the mistakes to avoid, you can be more confident about the decisions you need to make.

DON'T PROCRASTINATE.

If the decision to participate in a retirement savings plan is up to you, don't wait. Any money you invest today can potentially be worth more in the future than any money you wait to invest tomorrow. Even if you put in the maximum in later years, you won't be able to make up for lost time. And unless you participate, you won't be eligible for any matching funds your employer may provide.

DON'T BE TOO CAUTIOUS.

One of the greatest drags on retirement income is a portfolio of very safe investments whose returns lag behind others that pose only a moderately greater risk. Consider branching out from investments you're comfortable with to others offered in the plan that may have a history of stronger returns. By diversifying your investments, you can buffer your return from the periodic ups and downs that affect more volatile investments.

DON'T BE SHORT-SIGHTED.

The more time there is until you plan to retire, the less important the daily ups and downs of the investment market become. Since you generally can't withdraw the money before you turn 59½ without paying a penalty in any case, you may as well ignore occasional drops in market value, and set your sights on long-term results.

CHANGING TIMES

The evolution of defined contribution plans has been marked by constant change. Since 1974, when ERISA laid out the retirement plan regulations for employers and defined specific rights for employees, there have been more than 15 Congressional actions and dozens of IRS rulings that have modified one provision or another, sometimes making them more restrictive, and sometimes more flexible.

These changes range from the amount you can contribute and what you can withdraw without penalty, to whether you must take the initiative to participate or can be enrolled automatically.

In some cases, advantages that once existed but have been eliminated are still available to people who were part of a plan at the time those rules applied. That's a practice known as grandfathering. In other cases, the restrictions, such as contribution limits, apply across the board.

If you've been in the workforce 20 years or more and you are approaching retirement, you may want to get some expert professional advice on the rules that apply to you.

Tax-Deferred Investing

Cultivating tax-deferred investments is a way to provide cash crops when you retire.

Tax-deferred investment accounts have a major advantage that other investment accounts do not. You can postpone income tax on earnings until you withdraw money from your account.

What's more, you owe no tax on capital gains you might realize from selling investments in the tax-deferred account. That means you can reinvest the entire amount of any realized gain in the value of your investments, and you don't have to share any of your profit with the IRS.

For example, if you bought 200 shares of stock in your tax-deferred account for $20 a share and the price increased to $100 a share, you could sell and reinvest the entire $20,000. In contrast, in a taxable account, you'd owe $4,000 in capital gains tax (assuming you'd held the stock for a year and you pay a 20% capital gains tax rate) and would have only $16,000 left to reinvest. (Commissions on the trades would be subtracted in both cases.) You can continue to sell and reinvest for as long as your account is open, taking advantage of increases in investment value and opportunities for new investment.

Over the long term, postponing tax on earnings and capital gains creates the potential for significant growth in your tax-deferred account.

TYPES OF PLANS

There are various types of tax-deferred plans, including:
- Individual retirement accounts (IRAs)
- Individual annuities
- Employer sponsored retirement savings plans, including 401(k)s, 403(b)s, simplified employee pension plans (SEPs), and Keoghs

All of these plans are similar in that investments you make with money you put into the plans can grow tax deferred. And in each case, you owe a 10% penalty plus the income tax that's due for taking money out of the account before you turn 59½—though there are some situations when the penalty may not apply.

But there are some important differences among these tax-deferred plans as well, resulting from the federal laws that govern their operation. Those differences include the source of the money you contribute, whether or not you're required to begin taking money out of your account by a certain date, and whether those withdrawals are taxed.

IRAs

Contribution from earned income only	Yes
Contribution limit	Yes
Required withdrawal	Yes, traditional IRA No, Roth IRA
Tax due on withdrawal	Yes, traditional IRA No, Roth IRA
Funded by	You

PLAYING THE TAX GAME

You pay income tax on money you withdraw from your tax-deferred accounts at whatever your tax rate is for the year you withdraw. For example, if your adjusted gross income, including the amount you've withdrawn, puts you in the 28% bracket, that's the top rate at which you pay tax, and the one that will apply to your withdrawal amount.

You may wonder if you'll end up owing more tax on the money you eventually take out of your tax-deferred account than

[15%] [28%] [31%] [36%] [39.6%]

Your marginal tax rate is the highest rate at which you pay federal income tax. Rates go up as your taxable income increases.

SPLITTING HAIRS

While you'll hear lots of talk about tax-deferred investments, it's actually the account or, in the case of a retirement savings plan, the plan that's tax-deferred. Any earnings on money you've contributed are tax-deferred because the investments are held in the account or plan.

That's why an investment might be tax-deferred if purchased with money you've put into a 401(k) plan, but not tax-deferred if you bought that same investment for your taxable investment portfolio.

ANNUITY CONTRACTS	EMPLOYER SPONSORED PLANS
No	Yes
No	Yes
No. No federal rules apply. Individual states or annuity providers may require withdrawals at some point.	Yes
Yes	Yes
You	You, your employer, sometimes both

you would have paid in tax at the time you earned the money. Realistically, there's no way to tell. Tax rates change over time, depending on a number of factors. What you earn changes as well. That means you might have more income after you retire than in many of the years you contributed to a tax-deferred plan. But, despite the uncertainty, most experts agree that there's no better way for most people to build a retirement account than to take advantage of tax-deferred plans.

SETTING THE RECORD STRAIGHT

Did you ever wonder why a tax-deferred investment earns more than the same investment in a taxable account? Actually, it doesn't. But the earnings aren't the issue. Your bottom line is.

For example, suppose that on the same day you bought $2,000 worth of mutual fund shares for your tax-deferred IRA and $2,000 worth of shares in the same mutual fund as a regular, taxable investment. Suppose, too, that you had the earnings reinvested, and you left the investments alone for ten years. What you'd discover is that both accounts would have exactly the same value. So, you might ask, what is all the fuss about?

It's taxes. Each year during the ten-year period, you would have owed income tax on all the earnings that were reinvested in the taxable account. As long as you had enough on hand to pay your bill, or you could offset any capital gain with investment losses, you could let your investment compound. But whatever you paid in taxes would reduce the amount you had available to spend or invest elsewhere.

In contrast, you'd owe no tax on the sheltered account during the ten years. In fact, if you didn't withdraw for 30 years, you'd owe no tax during that period either. That means more money in your pocket.

Retirement Plans

A qualified retirement plan is a special breed.

When a 401(k), profit sharing plan, or pension plan is described as **qualified**, it means that it's an employer sponsored plan that gets special tax benefits because it meets a set of government regulations.

Those benefits apply to your employer, who gets a tax deduction for any contributions the company makes to the plan. The benefits also apply to you as a plan participant. You get to postpone income taxes on the money you and your employer contribute to your account until you withdraw it—even if that doesn't happen for 50 years. A qualified plan also lets you defer taxes on any earnings those contributions produce.

Employers who offer qualified plans to all eligible employees may also offer nonqualified plans to attract or hold onto certain key employees. These plans, known as excess or top-hat plans, aren't governed by the ERISA rules requiring that everyone be treated alike.

EQUALITY UNDER THE LAW

Among the most important regulations governing qualified plans are those that require an employer to cover substantially all employees and not discriminate in favor of higher-paid employees.

That generally means that all employees are eligible to participate on the same terms. If one full-time employee who has worked for a company for a year is eligible for the plan, then so are all the other full-time employees who have been on the job the same amount of time.

Employers must calculate contributions in an equitable way for everyone who participates. If a company contributes 10% of

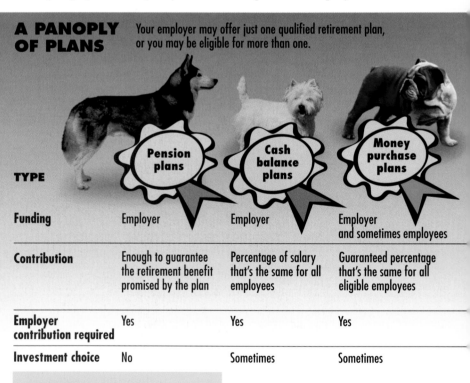

A PANOPLY OF PLANS

Your employer may offer just one qualified retirement plan, or you may be eligible for more than one.

TYPE	Pension plans	Cash balance plans	Money purchase plans
Funding	Employer	Employer	Employer and sometimes employees
Contribution	Enough to guarantee the retirement benefit promised by the plan	Percentage of salary that's the same for all employees	Guaranteed percentage that's the same for all eligible employees
Employer contribution required	Yes	Yes	Yes
Investment choice	No	Sometimes	Sometimes

CHANGING THE RULES

Some big changes to retirement savings plans were introduced in Congress during 2000, but hadn't been passed at year's end. Among the changes you're likely to enjoy are increased contribution levels for all types of plans, catch-up provisions in all employer sponsored plans, and the right to transfer assets between different plans.

QUALIFIED EXCEPTIONS

There are three other types of retirement savings plans that share many of the characteristics of a 401(k), though they are not technically qualified plans. These include:

- 403(b)s, also known as tax-sheltered annuities (TSAs) or tax-deferred annuities (TDAs), offered by schools, hospitals, and other nonprofits one employee's salary to a profit sharing plan, for example, it must contribute 10% of another eligible employee's salary. Similarly, if one employee can contribute up to 10% of his or her salary to a 401(k), then all employees must be eligible to contribute up to 10% as well.

The only exception to this rule works against highly paid employees, a category that includes anyone earning $85,000 or more in 2000. Their contribution rate may be limited if not enough lower-paid employees participate or if they contribute only a small percentage of their income.

Of course, employers are free to find other ways to reward company executives or other employees—using stock options, salary increases, or other non-qualified retirement plans.

If your employer establishes a non-qualified plan to benefit key employees, funding for the account isn't part of your salary, so you don't owe income tax until you eventually withdraw from the plan. The drawbacks, though, are that you're unlikely to collect if you leave your job, and the assets aren't protected from your employer's creditors, or from yours.

A DIFFERENT APPROACH

Like a qualified plan, certain **nonqualified** retirement savings plans give you the advantage of tax-deferred earnings. The difference is that your contribution to the plan must be in after-tax dollars—that is, money on which you have already paid income tax. But despite that lack of tax savings, nonqualified plans have some appealing features.

Annuity contracts, for example, offer added flexibility in several areas. The money you put into an annuity doesn't have to be earned income. That allows you to shelter an inheritance, money from the sale of a business, or other lump sum.

If you put money into a nondeductible IRA, you can invest up to $2,000 of your earned income each year in almost any investments you choose. Roth IRAs provide a source of tax-free income any time after you reach 59½, provided your account has been open at least five years.

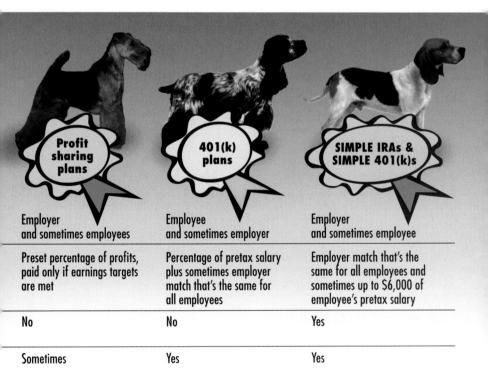

Profit sharing plans	401(k) plans	SIMPLE IRAs & SIMPLE 401(k)s
Employer and sometimes employees	Employee and sometimes employer	Employer and sometimes employee
Preset percentage of profits, paid only if earnings targets are met	Percentage of pretax salary plus sometimes employer match that's the same for all employees	Employer match that's the same for all employees and sometimes up to $6,000 of employee's pretax salary
No	No	Yes
Sometimes	Yes	Yes

- 457 plans, which are offered by state and local governments
- Thrift savings plans, which are offered by the federal government
  With these plans, as with a 401(k), eligible employees can contribute a percentage of their pretax salary to the plan, and all eligible employees can participate at the same level. Each plan offers partici-

pants a choice of investments, though some have a more limited selection menu than others. In some cases, employers match contributions.

While such a plan is sometimes offered as a supplement to a defined benefit plan, assets invested in these plans are likely to be the primary source of retirement income for most participants.

Salary Reduction Plans

Reducing your salary doesn't take much effort, and it's great for your financial health.

Salary reduction plans work for you in two ways.

First, part of what you earn is subtracted from your gross income before your earnings are reported to federal and most state income tax agencies. So you owe less tax than you would on your full salary. That puts money in your pocket—or better yet, in an investment account you open with that money.

Second, the pretax income that's withheld can be invested in a **tax-deferred savings plan**, such as a 401(k), to help improve your chances of enjoying a financially secure retirement. Or, the money can go into a **flexible spending account** if your employer offers that option as part of your benefits package.

STAY FLEXIBLE

Flexible spending accounts, offered as part of a cafeteria plan, also let you contribute pretax income you can use to pay for qualifying expenses, including medical costs that aren't covered by insurance, child care, and care for elderly or disabled dependents. Your employer will probably set a limit on what you can set aside, and you do have to spend the money in the account before the end of the year.

But you don't want to pass up this opportunity to save while you spend. You don't owe any income tax on the pretax amounts you put into this account.

NUTS AND BOLTS

When you're part of a salary reduction plan, you choose the percentage of your earnings that will go into your retirement savings account. That percentage, multiplied by your actual gross salary for the pay period, produces the dollar amount by

A Good Deal

There's no easier way to reduce your income taxes or build a retirement savings account than with a salary reduction plan. The more pretax income

The more money you put in a 401(k) plan...

401(k)

By taking advantage of a salary reduction plan, you lower your taxes while you invest for retirement

By not taking advantage of a salary reduction plan, you pay more in tax and risk having nothing invested for retirement

the lower your taxable salary...

TAXABLE INCOME

$75,000	Salary
– $6,000	Salary reduction
= $69,000	Taxable income

$75,000	Salary
– $0	Salary reduction
= $75,000	Taxable income

which your salary is reduced—and the amount that's added to your 401(k).

For example, if your gross salary is $2,500 twice a month and you contribute 10% of it to your 401(k), you add $250 to your account each time you're paid, or $6,000 for the year. The $250 is subtracted before income taxes are withheld, so less is taken out. And the $6,000 is not reported as income, so you report a smaller amount than you actually earned when you file your tax return. However, the amount you owe for Social Security and Medicare is figured on your gross salary.

The money that's withheld typically goes briefly into a holding account that your employer maintains, and then into the investments you've chosen. The holding accounts may pay some interest—perhaps 3% to 5% annually or 0.25% to 0.42% monthly—which is allocated proportionally to you and other plan participants, based on your share of the total assets.

Your employer must move the amounts that have been withheld into your investment account within 15 days of the end of the month it was withheld, so the amount is invested quickly. Allocating money from each paycheck to your 401(k) lets you use the investment strategy known as **dollar cost averaging**. That

means you are investing a fixed amount of money on a regular schedule. If the price of the investment changes—as the share price of a mutual fund typically does—you buy more shares when the price drops and fewer shares when it increases. But over time, your average cost per share is less than the average price per share.

HOW MUCH CAN YOU SHED?

There are limits on the amount of income you can contribute to a salary reduction plan each year. Congress establishes one ceiling—a dollar amount—and your employer sets another—usually a percentage of your salary. The total that you and your employer together can add to your account for 2001 is 25% of pay, or $35,000, whichever is less.

you contribute, the less tax you owe and the greater your account's potential for growth. For example, if you can reduce your $75,000 salary by 8% by contributing to a salary reduction plan, you'll owe $1,860 less in federal income tax and you'll add $6,000 to your 401(k).

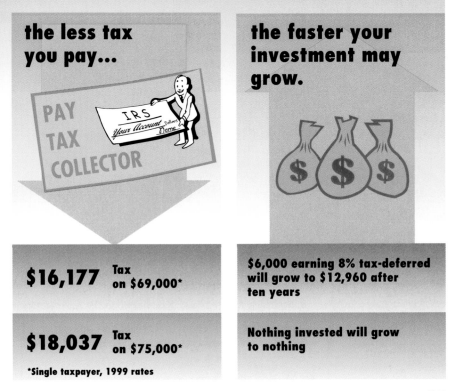

the less tax you pay...

PAY TAX COLLECTOR

$16,177 Tax on $69,000*

$18,037 Tax on $75,000*

*Single taxpayer, 1999 rates

the faster your investment may grow.

$6,000 earning 8% tax-deferred will grow to $12,960 after ten years

Nothing invested will grow to nothing

401(k) Plans

You direct your 401(k), but every plan has people behind the scenes.

Even though your 401(k) account is set up in your name, and the money you contribute is yours, the account itself is just one of many in your employer's plan. And that plan is just one of the thousands of plans operating in the US.

It will probably come as no surprise that even the smallest plan has several layers of management, to handle the regulations imposed by ERISA.

Some of those administrative tasks affect you only indirectly, such as monitoring the plan and filing reports to make sure the plan is operating within federal guidelines. But other plan details may have a direct impact on how easily and effectively you'll be able to build your retirement assets. For example, they require that you're given enough information to make informed decisions.

Of course, not every plan is the same. Many companies hire outside professionals for most of the tasks, though larger companies may establish special departments to handle them. Some of the roles may be consolidated. But all the jobs have to get done or the plan itself may be in jeopardy.

SETTING DIRECTION

Every 401(k) plan has a **sponsor**, who is almost always your employer. In larger companies, there is generally a person or management group responsible for initiating the plan, deciding on its structure and features, and delegating the task of running it.

The sponsor decides how long you must wait to join the plan, the percentage of salary that you can contribute, and all of the other plan features that are not dictated by law. In fact, the sponsor can automatically sign you up for the plan, so you must elect not to participate if you don't want to. That's a change from past practice, when there was no **negative enrollment**, and you had to take the initiative to join.

The sponsor also chooses, either directly or indirectly, the menu of investments the plan will offer. For example, in designating a particular investment manager for the plan, the sponsor may in effect be agreeing to offer a specific family of mutual funds or annuity funds. Or the sponsor might take the additional step of selecting some individual funds from among those the manager offers.

The sponsor also oversees withholding money from your salary and transferring that money to your 401(k) plan, along with any matching contribution the company makes. And any decision to end the plan is made by the sponsor as well.

PLAN PROVIDERS

Once a plan sponsor decides to offer a 401(k), the next task is choosing a **plan provider**. That may be a mutual fund company, insurance company, brokerage firm, bank, or other financial services company that offers investment products and recordkeeping services. The provider may also be an administrative specialist such as a benefit consulting firm or accounting firm that puts together a package of investment products from a number of different sources. Or the provider may

SO WHAT'S A PLAN FIDUCIARY?

A fiduciary is someone who's responsible for making financial or plan management decisions in the best interests of the people who will benefit from those decisions. For example, one of a 401(k) plan sponsor's key fiduciary responsibilities is selecting appropriate investments that offer you a real menu of real choices. If you're given reasonable alternatives, you can't hold your plan sponsor responsible for disappointing results or for your having selected certain investments over others.

be an institutional investment manager or adviser who designs investment strategies and offers private-label investments.

What the sponsor is looking for in a plan provider is an organization or group of affiliated organizations that will:

- Provide strong investment choices
- Offer investor education and retirement planning
- Handle recordkeeping and process loan applications or hardship withdrawals
- Monitor the plan to be sure it complies with federal requirements
- Provide the service at a reasonable cost

HANDLING THE JOB

Each 401(k) plan needs someone inside the company to keep things running smoothly, whether or not the sponsor uses an outside company to handle most of the management details. That person is your **plan manager**. You can go to your plan manager for answers to questions about when you qualify to join, the contribution rate that lets you make the most of a company match, or the procedures to apply for a loan.

Unless your plan is self-trusteed, you're unlikely to encounter the plan's **trustee**, usually a bank, mutual fund, or other financial institution that holds your contribution, and the contributions of other employees in trust, and allocates them to the investments you've chosen. Nor are you likely meet with the **investment manager**, the person or group who is responsible for the investments that the plan makes available to you.

WHEN IT WORKS RIGHT

The best evidence that your 401(k) is well run is that it works smoothly. Your account statements arrive on time, you can tell that your contributions are being added on a regular basis according to the instructions you've given, and any questions or requests you have get answered promptly.

403(b) Plans

Retirement plans may share a family resemblance, but they're not mirror images.

If you work for a nonprofit, tax-exempt organization, your employer is more likely to sponsor a 403(b) retirement savings plan than a 401(k) plan, though some nonprofits do offer 401(k)s.

Like their 401(k) cousins, 403(b) plans are named for the sections of the IRS code that authorize this type of plan. In addition, from a participant's perspective 403(b) and 401(k) plans are similar in several important ways. For example, both:

- Let you contribute pretax income and accumulate tax-deferred earnings
- Are usually self-directed, which means you're responsible for making investment decisions
- Require you to begin taking money out of your plan when you turn 70½ (in most cases)
- Pay income tax on those withdrawals at your regular income tax rate

But the plans also have significant differences. One of the most important is the type of investments you're allowed to make. Another is that 403(b) plans have a catch-up provision, which allows you to make up for lost contributions if you did not participate in the plan when you first became eligible. The eligibility rules are complicated, however, so you'll need to work with your plan administrator to find out if you qualify, how much you might be able to add to your account, and the timetable for making the additional contributions.

TO THE LIMIT

When you contribute to a 403(b) plan, you typically agree to reduce your take-home pay by a certain percentage and to deposit that amount into a tax-deferred account. The income tax you owe is reduced as well, since the amount you defer is not reported to the IRS as current earnings.

403(b)

- Matching contributions not common
- You have a $10,500 contribution cap or a MEA, whichever is less
- You are 100% vested from the time of deposit
- Your account is not covered by ERISA rules

Though your employer has the right to match your contribution, or make contributions to the plan on some other basis, matching isn't as common with 403(b) plans as it is with 401(k)s. There are two key reasons. One is that your 403(b) may be offered in addition to a traditional defined benefit retirement plan. Another is that employers who do contribute must assume fiduciary responsibility for the plan investments, as 401(k) sponsors do. That's no simple matter, so they may simply elect to avoid matching contributions altogether.

As a participant in a 403(b), you can defer either up to $10,500 in 2001—the same cap as a 401(k)—or what's known as your maximum exclusion allowance (MEA), whichever is less. Your MEA depends on the number of years you've held your job, the amount you earn, and all previous contributions you've made to the plan. You should consult your plan's manager to determine which limit to use.

THIS IS YOUR PLAN

If your retirement plan is a tax-sheltered annuity (TSA) or a tax-deferred annuity (TDA), it's actually a 403(b). In fact, the language of the law establishing 403(b)s says that the money you put into the plan will buy an annuity for your retirement.

If you do switch your account to another provider, you may run into some red tape and perhaps have to pay some surrender fees. And you should check regularly to be sure that the contributions you're deferring are being invested as you wish. But if you're more satisfied with the new investment options than with the ones available through your employer's plan, you may find that making the switch is worth the hassle.

401(k)

- Matching contributions are usually made by your employer
- You have a $10,500 contribution cap
- You are vested after a certain time period
- Your account is covered by ERISA rules

GETTING YOUR MONEY OUT

With a 403(b) plan, you must usually begin required withdrawals at 70½, though if you put money into your plan before 1987, you may be able to wait until you're 75.

As with a 401(k), you must pay a 10% early withdrawal penalty in addition to the income tax that's due for taking money out of your account before you're 59½. There are exceptions, though, if you leave your job after you turn 55, or if you arrange to take a series of essentially equal withdrawals over a period of at least five years or until you turn 59½, whichever period is longer.

When you leave your job for any reason, you can roll over your 403(b) assets into an IRA or another employer's 403(b) plan. And when you retire, you can move your account balance to an IRA or leave it in the plan.

When you begin taking minimum required withdrawals from a 403(b), you figure the amount you must take based on your account's value at the end of the previous year and your official life expectancy. The dollar amount of those withdrawals may vary from year to year, based on the return your investments provide. But the process is designed to ensure that the entire value of your account will be paid out during your lifetime or the joint lifetimes of you and your beneficiary.

PUTTING MONEY IN

When contributing to a 403(b), you can choose between two categories of investments: annuities—either fixed or variable—or mutual funds. No other choices are allowed.

One important benefit of a 403(b) is that you're 100% vested in the assets in your plan from the time your deferred salary is deposited into your account. And, if all the contributions in your account are from your pretax salary, you have the right to transfer the assets that accumulate in your account out of the investments offered by your plan provider and into different investments offered by another 403(b) annuity or mutual fund provider.

The advantage of being able to switch your investments is that you may find choices with stronger returns or lower fees than those offered through your employer's plan. This flexibility helps counter a persistent criticism of many, though not all, 403(b) plans as being too limiting and too fee-heavy.

457 Plans

Understanding different retirement savings plans is a numbers game.

If you work for a state or local government, or for some nonprofit organizations, your employer may sponsor a section 457 retirement savings plan. These plans, like 401(k) and 403(b) plans, are named for the section of the IRS code that describes how they operate and who is eligible to participate.

All three types of plans share some basic features, including the right to contribute pretax income and accumulate tax-deferred earnings. They also give plan participants the responsibility to make investment decisions, and require minimum withdrawals when you turn 70½.

But 457 plans are also distinctively different from either 401(k)s or 403(b)s. Among the most important features that set them apart are

- The amount you can contribute each year
- Your right to the assets in the account
- Your ability to make catch-up contributions
- The rules governing early and required distributions

CONTRIBUTION RULES

A 457 plan is a deferred compensation plan. To participate, you typically agree to postpone taking part of your current salary until you leave your job. At that time, you'll have the right to collect the amount you allocated to the plan, plus any tax-deferred earnings it has produced. As an added incentive, the amount you defer isn't reported as income to the IRS, reducing the tax you owe.

In 2001, the most you can put into your 457 plan is $8,000—less than the $10,500 cap on 401(k)s and 403(b)s. However, if you didn't put in the maximum amount each previous year you were eligible, you may be able to make contributions above the cap during the final three years before you reach normal retirement age.

IT'S YOURS...EVENTUALLY

When you participate in a 457 plan, the part of your salary you agree to contribute to the plan doesn't actually belong to you until you leave your job or retire.

Technically, all of a 457 plan's assets are owned by the plan sponsor, and they're held in trust for you in an account set up in your name.

But the decisions about how the money is invested is still yours to make, and the eventual value of your account depends on your investment choices. You can select any of the options offered through the plan. You're not restricted to annuities and mutual funds, as 403(b) participants are, but in reality many plan providers offer only those choices.

GETTING YOUR MONEY OUT

The rules that govern required distributions from a 457 plan resemble the rules for 401(k)s and 403(b)s in one important way: You must begin taking money out of your account by April 1 of the year following the year you turn 70½ and pay income tax at your regular income tax rate on the amount you take. But that's where the similarities end.

With a 457 plan, your required withdrawals must be calculated to pay a minimum of two-thirds of the account balance over your life expectancy, rather than the 100% that 401(k) and 403(b) plans officially require. And once you begin taking distributions, you must take an equal dollar amount each year. For example, if the minimum required distribution was $10,000 for the year you turned 70½, you'd have to take $10,000 each year after that.

There are other differences, as well. Unlike the 10% penalty you may face for taking money out of a 401(k) or 403(b) before you reach 59½, as a 457 participant you owe no penalty if your money is paid to you when you leave your job, no matter what your age is.

On the downside, however, you have one less way to maintain the tax-deferred status of your retirement savings when you leave your job or when you retire. When you're part of a 401(k) or a 403(b) plan, you can roll over the account value into an IRA. But that alternative isn't available with a 457 plan.

Since an IRA rollover is not an option, you must decide within 60 days after you leave your job whether to keep your money in the 457 plan, take a lump-sum distribution, set up a payment schedule, or move the money to a new employer's 457 plan. If you miss the deadline, you'll owe income tax on the entire amount that the plan holds in your name, even if you haven't received any of the money.

NO EARLY WITHDRAWAL PENALTY FOR 457

THE NATURE OF TRUST

Although 457 plans are deferred compensation plans, the money you've put into the plan is secured in an irrevocable trust, also known as a secular trust. The trust guarantees that you'll collect retirement income from your plan—protecting your assets against both your employer's creditors and the possibility that your employer might be unwilling or unable to find the cash when payout time comes.

In contrast, a rabbi trust holds assets an employer may set aside to pay deferred compensation that's been promised to employees—typically those that are already highly paid—as supplemental tax-deferred retirement income. From the employee's point of view, there's less protection than with a secular trust, since a rabbi trust does not insulate assets in the trust from creditors if the employer's business fails.

RETIREMENT SOUP

CONTRIBUTIONS	401(k)	403(b)	457
$10,500 limit	✓	✓	
$8,000 limit			✓

WITHDRAWALS	401(k)	403(b)	457
Leave in plan	Yes	Yes	Yes
Take lump sum	Yes	Yes	Yes
Take payments	Yes	Yes	Yes
Rollover to IRA	Yes	Yes	No
New employer plan	Yes	Yes	Yes

Individual Retirement Accounts

You can find an IRA that's the right style for you.

Individual retirement accounts (IRAs) are tax-deferred retirement savings accounts you set up on your own. You can contribute up to $2,000 of your employment earnings each year, even if you're contributing to a 401(k) or other salary reduction plan or are enrolled in a traditional defined benefit plan.

But IRAs become a particularly important tool if you leave your job for any reason. You can roll over, or transfer, the value of your account to an IRA in your name. Taking that action preserves the tax-deferred status of your contributions and any earnings they may have produced.

Though you may have the option of moving those assets to a new employer's plan, you can choose instead to leave the money in your rollover IRA. Either way, any earnings can compound tax deferred.

IT'S YOUR ACCOUNT

You open an IRA by filling out an application provided by the mutual fund company, brokerage firm, bank, or other financial services company you choose as custodian or trustee of your account.

There's typically a small annual fee to handle your account—often between $10 and $50—though it may be waived when your account value reaches the custodian's minimum, perhaps $5,000 to $10,000. That's one reason most advisers suggest you consolidate your IRA accounts rather than keeping several small ones open.

If you're contributing earned income to your IRA each year, you can put money into the account on a schedule that suits you, whether once a week or once a year. Your custodian follows your instructions for investing the money, provides regular account summaries, and sends an annual report of what you've contributed for the year. But the rest of the responsibility is yours, including being sure you don't contribute more than the limit.

2003: THE WITHDRAWAL

If you opened a Roth IRA the first year they were available—1998—you'll have to wait until 2003 to withdraw tax-free earnings. And you'll have to be at least 59½ to avoid a penalty and taxes.

A GALLERY OF IRAs

The term IRA is actually used to describe several different types of accounts that are the same in some ways, but different in others.

1 TRADITIONAL IRAs

Traditional IRAs may be nondeductible or deductible. The difference affects whether the contribution you make is taxed now or later.

You can deduct your IRA contribution from your gross income only if you don't participate in a retirement plan at work or your income is less than an annual minimum set by Congress.

You must begin taking required withdrawals when you turn 70½.

If you qualify, you can convert your traditional IRA to a Roth IRA by paying the tax that's due on both your accumulated earnings and on your contributions if you deducted them.

2 ROTH IRAs

Roth IRAs are always nondeductible but are designed to provide tax-free income.

You can contribute to a Roth IRA only if your income is less than the amount set by Congress.

You aren't required to withdraw from your account at 70½ (or ever) if you don't want to.

Any withdrawals you do make are free of income tax if you're older than 59½ and your account has been open at least five years.

3 ROLLOVER IRAs

Rollover IRAs are traditional IRAs with a few special features.

You can move money you've accumulated in any qualified retirement plan or 403(b) into a rollover IRA and preserve your money's tax-deferred status.

It's important, though, to keep a rollover IRA separate from a traditional IRA. If you do, the rollover is considered a conduit IRA, and you may be eligible to move the assets into a new employer's salary reduction plan. Figuring the income tax that's due may also be more complicated if you mix assets from two types of IRAs.

You must begin required withdrawals when you reach 70½.

DUAL ACCOUNTS

If you and your spouse are both employed, each of you can contribute up to $2,000 to your own IRA. If your husband or wife doesn't earn income, but you do, you can contribute to your own account and a second $2,000 to a spousal account.

If your adjusted gross income (AGI) is less than $150,000, you can deduct the amount you put into a traditional spousal IRA or choose a Roth IRA for your spouse. Once the account is established, it's the property of your spouse.

UNCLE SAM WANTS TO KNOW

You must report your IRA contribution to the IRS. The information goes on your basic tax return if it's a deductible contribution, or on Form 8606 if it's not. Your retirement savings plan administrator will report any money you moved out of your employer's plan. Similarly, your IRA custodian will report money you move from your account, and the custodians of any new IRAs will report any deposits that are made.

Even though you may be tempted to weed out your tax records from time to time, don't throw out any IRA-related information. You may need to be able to prove that you met required rollover deadlines, kept certain deposits separate from others, and paid tax on the contributions you didn't deduct. Otherwise, you may risk being doubly taxed or incur other penalties.

Mapping Your Future

You can think of joining a 401(k) plan as starting out on a great adventure.

The best reason for putting money in a 401(k) is that it can help put you on the road to long-term financial security. Reaching that goal is primarily your job, not the government's or your employer's.

To participate, you fill out an enrollment form, call a toll-free number, or enroll online. When you enroll, you authorize your employer to withhold a certain percentage of your gross pay as your contribution to the plan. In self-directed plans, you choose specific investments offered through the plan and indicate how the amount that's withheld should be divided among them.

Your contribution is invested in your account, based on the investments and allocations you've indicated. For example, if your plan offers mutual funds, you might select three and divide your contribution evenly among them, or you might put half the amount in one of the funds and split the remaining half evenly between the other two.

TAX WISE

Remember that 401(k)s are salary reduction plans. So every dollar you contribute reduces your taxable income by a dollar. And though you give up access to the money while you're investing, you may actually end up with more money in your pocket now as well as later.

For example, if you subtract a $7,200 annual contribution from your gross income, you reduce your federal income taxes by $2,000 to $3,000, based on your filing status and your total income. You'll probably pay less in state income tax as well. And the more you contribute, the more your gross salary is reduced and the greater your tax savings.

Of course, the smartest thing to do with the extra cash is to invest it, too, either in a tax-deferred individual retirement account (IRA), or in taxable investments. Your tax savings may also come in handy to meet unexpected bills, or to pay for something that's important to you.

TIME CAN MULTIPLY EARNINGS

There's a lot to be said for contributing early and often to a tax-deferred retirement savings plan. Because you don't have to pay any income taxes on the earnings in your account, your investment **compounds** untaxed. That means any earnings are added to your original investment to form a new investment base. As a result, your return may compound on a larger base each year. And, if you keep contributing year after year, you're adding still more to the expanding base.

Suppose you open your account on the first day of the year by contributing $300 and add $300 from each paycheck. If you get paid twice a month, by year's end you'll have contributed $7,200 ($300 times 24 paychecks).

Let's assume your contribution buys shares of a mutual fund that cost an average of $15. This means you add 20 shares each pay period, or a total of 480 for the year, and reinvest your earnings. With an 8% return, you'd start the next year with a total of 518.4 shares, all of them generating earnings.

The rate at which growth takes place varies from year to year, and there's always the possibility that your account could lose value. But over time, compounding can produce significant investment returns.

For example, if you put $7,200 into your 401(k) plan each year for 30 years, or $216,000, and your earnings compound at 8% annually—an historically realistic rate if you put at least 60% of your assets into equity investments, including stock mutual funds—you'll accumulate an account worth approximately $900,177. Although you'll have to pay income tax at your ordinary rate when you withdraw, you'll still have a substantial amount of money.

HOW COMPOUNDING WORKS

You invest $7,200 annually with an 8% rate of return	Compounded amount
Year 1	$7,470
Year 10	$110,499
Year 20	$355,768
Year 30	$900,177

Investment
Choices
Forest

START HERE

Tax River

RETIREMENT

IN TIMELY FASHION

By law, your employer is required to invest your contributions no later than 15 business days after the end of the month in which the money is deducted from your paycheck. The deadline can be extended another 10 business days if your employer notifies you that there will be a delay and meets certain other legal requirements.

THE MAGIC NUMBERS

The deal you make with the government when you contribute to a 401(k) is that you'll get tax-deferred earnings and the government gets the right to a 10% penalty on any money you take out of your plan early. Basically that means any money you withdraw before you reach the age of 59½, though there are some exceptions.

After 59½, you can take as much money as you want each year. You'll owe income tax at your current tax rate on everything you withdraw except on any aftertax contributions you made, where the rules differ. But you're not required to take any money out until April 1 of the year following the year you turn 70½, more than 11 years later.

Do 59½ and 70½ strike you as curious ages to be such important turning points? The government uses them because according to the actuaries who calculate life expectancy, you're already 60 (a nice round age) when you turn 59½ and you're still 70 until you turn 70½.

MAKING CHANGES

When you tell your employer how much you want to contribute to your 401(k) or how you want your contribution invested, you're not making a lifelong commitment. You can increase or decrease the percentage of salary you're putting into the plan. And you can change your investment allocations as often as your plan allows, sometimes as often as once a day and rarely less frequently than once a quarter.

401(k)
Contribution

$

Your Income

Eligibility

The first requirement for winning the retirement savings race is qualifying to run.

The rules for qualifying to participate in a 401(k) are complex, but designed to give employees an equal opportunity to save for retirement. But you can't always start contributing to your employer's plan the day you start working. And in some cases you may not qualify at all.

One reason there is equality in 401(k) plans is that your employer must follow to the letter of the law the regulations that forbid discrimination, or risk having the entire plan disqualified. One of the key provisions is that your employer cannot give, or even seem to give, preference to higher-paid employees.

The government gives employers one escape clause. Since new and young employees have characteristically been the lowest paid and the least likely to join a 401(k) plan, employers have the right to postpone eligibility for new workers and exclude those under 21.

Enrollment Starts July 1!

A NEGOTIATED CONTRACT

About 40% of small employer plans and 57% of large employer plans already allow new hires to start contributing to 401(k) plans as soon as they start working.

So it pays to check the eligibility rules when considering a new job, and include immediate participation in the 401(k) plan as part of your deliberations.

Source: Profit Sharing/401(k) Council of America (PSCA), 2000.

THERE IS A SEASON

Being eligible to participate in a 401(k) doesn't necessarily mean you can actually start contributing. Some 401(k) plans have specific enrollment dates, such as January 1 and July 1, or an open season, such as the first two weeks in October. You can generally start contributions only at those times.

Suppose you start work on February 1, and your employer's 401(k) plan has a one-year waiting period with enrollment dates on January 1 and July 1. After a year on the job—the next February 1— you become eligible to contribute. But you must wait until July 1 to begin your contributions. That adds up to a 17 month wait.

An employer with no waiting period— which means you can start contributing as soon as you start the job—might still have entry dates or open seasons. In that case, if you start work on April 1, for example, you might still have to wait until the enrollment date on July 1.

EXCEPTIONS ARE THE RULE

If you're on the job when your employer offers a 401(k) plan for the first time, you may be eligible instantly—or at least as quickly as anyone else. That's likely to happen more often at small companies that add a plan to their benefits package when they reach a certain size and want to be able to attract and keep employees.

ON THE SIDELINES

Your employer does not have to allow you to participate in a 401(k) if you:

- Have been on the job less than a year
- Are younger than 21

But employers are increasingly willing to make exceptions to these exclusions. Those with existing plans may modify their plan descriptions to make newly hired employees eligible. And employers offering new plans may include them from the beginning. Among other things, that means that if you're changing jobs and want to move assets from your former employer's plan to your new employer's plan, you can do it right away.

The situation for employees younger than 21 is changing as well. Since 1999, employers can exclude participants younger than 21 when they do their nondiscrimination testing, provided that group of employees satisfies the minimum coverage requirements when tested separately. This modification in the law means that younger employees can contribute only a small percentage of pay if they wish without reducing the plan average.

ALTERNATE CHANNELS

If you can't start your 401(k) contributions right away, you don't qualify because you're too young, or you work for a company that doesn't offer a plan yet, you still may have some options to build your retirement savings.

While you're waiting, for example, you can contribute up to $2,000 of your earned income to an individual retirement account (IRA) or purchase a deferred annuity. Both alternatives offer the advantage of deferring income tax on any earnings those accounts may produce.

Many experts suggest investigating a Roth IRA if you're in this position. These IRAs provide tax-free income after you reach 59½, provided your account has been open at least five years.

Even though you won't be able to move IRA or annuity savings into your employer's plan when you are eligible to participate in a 401(k), you can keep your account open and even go on adding to it if you wish.

A WIN-WIN SITUATION

Your employer may actually be eager to reduce or even eliminate the waiting period, or relax the eligibility rules, if there's a risk that the company's 401(k) will be top heavy at the end of the plan year. That happens most frequently at small companies, when more than 60% of the assets in the plan belong to key personnel, such as the owner or members of the management team.

Encouraging an influx of new participants, and providing matching funds to help build their account values more quickly, can solve the problem. Large companies want full participation, too, so they can pass key nondiscrimination tests and let their higher paid employees contribute up to the full cap.

Your Company   You

Contribution Limits

You'll run up against a lid—or two—on the amount you can put into your 401(k).

Both the federal government and your employer limit the amount you can contribute to your 401(k) plan each year—though the limits they set differ.

The government sets a dollar limit on salary reductions, which is $10,500 for 2001. The cap increases in $500 increments, based on the Consumer Price Index (CPI). Your employer's cap is a percentage of what you earn on the job.

The percentage your employer allows you to contribute—which is typically 10% to 20% of your gross pay—may mean that the amount you can contribute is less than the government cap.

For example, if your employer sets the contribution rate at 15% of your salary, and you earn $60,000, the most you can contribute is $9,000 ($60,000 x .15 = $9,000), or any amount up to that. If you earn $30,000, you can contribute $4,500. On the other hand, if you earn $90,000 in 2001, you can't contribute the $13,500 that would be 15% of your salary because the government cap is $10,500.

The government doesn't set a floor, or minimum contribution, but many employers do require you to contribute a certain percentage of your salary, often 1% to 2%, if you're going to participate.

ANNUAL CONTRIBUTION CAPS

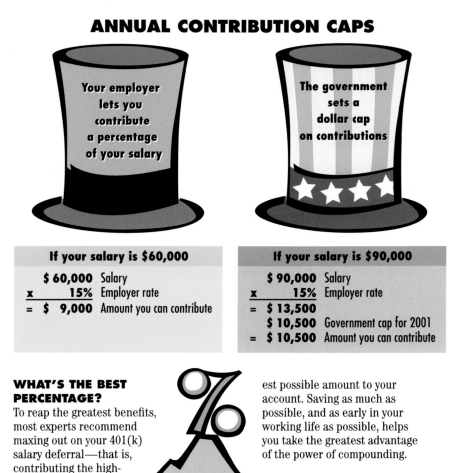

Your employer lets you contribute a percentage of your salary

The government sets a dollar cap on contributions

If your salary is $60,000

	$ 60,000	Salary
x	15%	Employer rate
=	$ 9,000	Amount you can contribute

If your salary is $90,000

	$ 90,000	Salary
x	15%	Employer rate
=	$ 13,500	
	$ 10,500	Government cap for 2001
=	$ 10,500	Amount you can contribute

WHAT'S THE BEST PERCENTAGE?

To reap the greatest benefits, most experts recommend maxing out on your 401(k) salary deferral—that is, contributing the high-est possible amount to your account. Saving as much as possible, and as early in your working life as possible, helps you take the greatest advantage of the power of compounding.

TAKING IT TO THE LIMIT(S)

To encourage companies to make their 401(k) plans attractive to all their employees—from support staff through top management—the government restricts the contributions that highly paid employees can make. Those limits affect anyone making $85,000 a year or more for 2000.

While the government's dollar cap doesn't change, the greatest average percentage of salary employees in the highly paid category can contribute is based on the average percentage the lower-paid employees are contributing. It may be two times the average percentage, two percentage points more than the average, or 1.25 times that average, based on what the average rate is.

Here's an example of how it works: If the average contribution of the employees earning less than $85,000 per year is 3% of their salaries, then the average percentage that those earning more than $85,000 can contribute is 5% (3% plus two percentage points). For example, someone making $90,000 might be able to

contribute $4,500 (5% of $90,000) instead of the $10,500 cap, which would amount to 11.65% of salary. And someone making $150,000 might be able to contribute $7,500 (5% of $150,000) instead of the 7% that would equal the $10,500 cap for 2001.

Furthermore, employees earning more than $170,000 in 2000 can't make 401(k) contributions or receive a company match on any earnings above that ceiling.

A STRANGE TWIST

If your salary is just under the $85,000 cutoff, you may be able to contribute more to your 401(k) than if your salary were just over that dividing line. That's because if you're under—even by a little—the 2% rule doesn't apply to you.

For example, if your salary is $84,000, your employer's contribution limit is 10%, and the average contribution for lower-paid workers is 4%, you could contribute 10%, or $8,400. But if you earned $86,000, you could contribute only 6%, or $5,160, because you'd be limited to contributing two percentage points more than the 4% average of the lower-paid workers.

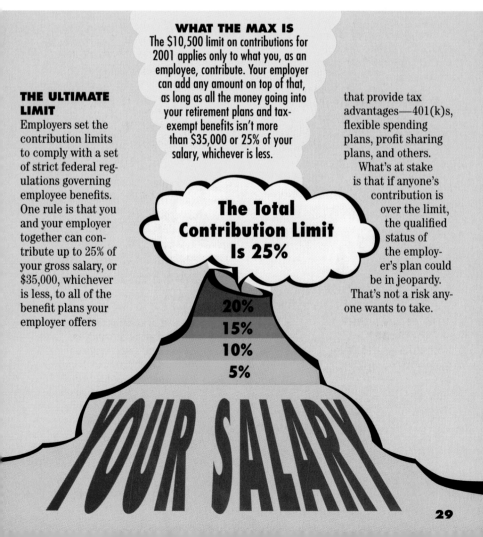

THE ULTIMATE LIMIT

Employers set the contribution limits to comply with a set of strict federal regulations governing employee benefits. One rule is that you and your employer together can contribute up to 25% of your gross salary, or $35,000, whichever is less, to all of the benefit plans your employer offers

WHAT THE MAX IS
The $10,500 limit on contributions for 2001 applies only to what you, as an employee, contribute. Your employer can add any amount on top of that, as long as all the money going into your retirement plans and tax-exempt benefits isn't more than $35,000 or 25% of your salary, whichever is less.

The Total Contribution Limit Is 25%

20%
15%
10%
5%

YOUR SALARY

that provide tax advantages—401(k)s, flexible spending plans, profit sharing plans, and others.

What's at stake is that if anyone's contribution is over the limit, the qualified status of the employer's plan could be in jeopardy. That's not a risk anyone wants to take.

Company Contributions

Here's the scoop: Matching contributions are a bonus.

If your employer matches, or adds to, the contributions you make to your retirement savings plans, think of it as a series of free gifts that continue to increase in value.

Employers aren't required to match contributions, but a majority of corporate employers do—up to a limit—especially when a 401(k) plan is the only retirement plan they offer. Not-for-profit and government employers offering similar savings plans may or may not match contributions, based on the kind of plan they offer and whether or not they also provide a pension.

VARIATIONS ON A THEME

Employers decide not only if they'll match your contributions but also the way their matches will be made. One common approach is to match 50% of what you contribute, or 50 cents for each dollar you put in, up to a maximum of 5% or 6% of your earnings. However, some employers match contributions dollar for dollar up to a certain percentage of your earnings—also often 6%, but sometimes more and sometimes less. Others put a dollar limit on the amount any employee can receive.

Some companies match employee contributions with shares of stock instead of cash. Or, they may require you to invest a certain amount of your 401(k) in company stock to be eligible for matching funds.

Regardless of their matching policy, employers must match funds equitably. For example, an employer can't match some employees' contributions to a limit of 3% of earnings and match other employees' contributions to a limit of 6%. But employers can match a higher percentage of contribution for people who've been employees for a certain period— say ten years—or for employees over a certain age. The other exception to this rule is that an employer can eliminate matches for highly compensated employees while matching contributions of lower-paid employees.

PAY, SET, MATCH

The pay that's eligible for a match depends on your plan's rules. Many employers use the same definition of pay for determining matching contributions that they use for determining salary reductions. Pay can be defined as your base salary, or as hourly wages plus overtime. Pay may also include any commissions or bonuses you receive.

WHAT'S GOOD FOR THE GOOSE

There are good business reasons for your employer to set up a matching plan. A generous 401(k) plan can help attract and keep valued staff. It can also encourage employees at all salary levels to participate in the plan, which means that higher-paid employees (including company executives) can contribute more to their own plans. And a portion of your employer's match provides a tax deduction for the company as well.

NO SURPRISE

If your 401(k) plan allows you to make aftertax contributions, you might qualify for matching funds on these amounts as well. But these matches are less common than those on pretax contributions.

CONTRIBUTION

COMPANY MATCH

50% of your contribution

TAKE WHAT YOU CAN GET

If you can't afford to invest the maximum in your 401(k), try to contribute at least enough to take full advantage of any company match.

ALL IN THE TIMING

Some employers deposit their matching contribution into your 401(k) account at the same time they deposit your contribution, whether it's every week, every two weeks, or every month. Other employers deposit their matching contributions monthly, quarterly, or annually.

If your employer matches your contributions through a profit-sharing plan, it's very important to know when the money actually goes into your account. If it's on the last day of the plan year for employees on the payroll on that day, you probably don't want to leave your job on the 27th—or any time in the last few days of the month. Wait, if possible, to get that last matching contribution. Otherwise, you're giving your employer a farewell gift.

And, if your employer is depositing matching contributions into your 401(k) account once a year, you're missing out on potential compounded earnings—11 months of matching for January, 10 months of matching for February, and so on. Your coworkers and supervisors are missing out, too. If your employer is open to negotiations, improving the timing of matching contributions is one way to get more out of your 401(k) plan.

GOT A MATCH?

Instead of—or, sometimes in addition to—regular matches linked to your contributions, your employer may add money to your 401(k) as part of a profit- or gain-sharing plan. In that case, the additional income you get—a percentage of your pay that may vary from year to year—is typically figured at the end of the year, based on the company's performance. (In fact, all employees may qualify for profit-sharing distributions whether or not they participate in a retirement savings plan.)

Matching contributions may also be on a sliding scale, depending on company profits, so your employer may match more of your contributions in some years than in others. Some plans also allow an employer to skip matching contributions in a given year, or reduce the matching amount in two years out of five.

TIME YOUR CONTRIBUTIONS

401(k)

Maxing Out Your Match

Making the most of matching contributions isn't always as easy as it would seem.

In general, it's smart to contribute the most you can to your 401(k), whether that amount is determined by the government cap or your employer's contribution limit. At the least, it's ideal if you can take full advantage of any employer's matching contribution. But, some highly paid employees may not be able to do both.

A MATCHING MISMATCH

In addition to establishing the percentage of your income they will match, employers calculate what they'll contribute based either on your total annual contribution or on your contribution in each pay period in accordance with the plan. While this might seem like a small difference, the impact on what you receive overall can add up.

For example, if you earn $90,000 and contribute 15% of your salary, you will reach the $10,500 maximum for 2001 in October, after earning $70,000. If your company matches 50% of your contribution each pay period up to 6% of the pay on which your contribution is based, you'll receive only $2,100 (50% of 6% of $70,000) for the year, instead of the $2,700 you would have been eligible for if the match had been based on your total salary (50% of 6% of $90,000).

There is a way around the problem. By lowering your contribution rate to 12%, you can space your contributions over the entire year and receive almost the full match. But you have to make that decision before the year starts.

If your salary is $90,000, and you contribute 15%, you'll hit the federal limit in October.
So you may receive less from your company match.

If you max out your contribution before the end of the year, you may be missing out on some matches.

NOT TO WORRY

Missing out on matching amounts isn't a problem everybody faces. To figure out if you risk losing some matching, divide the government's cap by the maximum percentage your employer allows.

For example, if you divide $10,500 by 15%, the result is $70,000. If you make that amount, you can contribute up to $10,500 and still qualify for all of the matching money your employer is likely to contribute. If the contribution rate is 10%, you can earn up to $105,000 and still contribute $10,500.

As a rule of thumb, the higher the contribution rate your employer allows and the higher your income, the more you need to pay attention to the rate at which you contribute. Before you select your contribution rate for the next year, review your account for the past year to be sure you got as much in matching funds as you were entitled to.

LATER IS BETTER THAN SOONER

There may also be a cap on the amount an employer will contribute in each pay period. This means you'll end up with more money if you spread out your contributions to qualify for matching instead of having your share taken out in big installments early in the year. For example, if you were earning $45,000 and your plan let you contribute 15% of your salary, or $6,750, you might consider doubling up your early contributions to put your money to work as quickly as possible. After all, that's what many financial advisers encourage you to do with individual retirement account (IRA) contributions.

But if your plan matches your contribution each pay period, it would be a mistake, since you'd reach your contribution limit early in the year. Your employer's match would stop when your contributions stopped. You might get as little as half of what you could have qualified for.

If you make a contribution every month, your employer may match every contribution you make.

If your salary is $90,000, and you contribute at a lower rate of 12% but contribute every month, you may receive more employer matching contributions.

THE OTHER SHOE

Sometimes there's no way to maximize both your contribution and your employer's match no matter how hard you try—though it happens only when your income is in the $170,000 range. At that level, if you contribute 6% of your salary, presuming that's the percentage your employer will match, your contribution for the year will total $10,200. You'll qualify for a match of $5,100 if your employer matches 50% of 6% of your earnings, but you'll fall short of the government cap.

The more you earn, the more creatively you have to plan in order to get the greatest benefit. That's because there's an annual limit on the earnings that qualify for 401(k) contributions. In 2001, it's any amount over $170,000—an amount that may be increased over time to reflect increases in inflation.

LAST MINUTE MATTERS

If your employer waits to match your contributions until the end of the year, the amount eligible for matching matters more than the rate at which you contributed.

SCHEDULE CHANGES

There may be times when you want to change your contribution rate, which you may be able to do online or by phone. Check to find out how long it will take to put your request into effect.

If you get a salary increase or a big bonus, you may have to reduce your rate to ensure that your total contribution doesn't exceed the dollar amount that's allowed for the year.

If you know you'll be leaving your current job, and won't be able to contribute to the 401(k) at your new one for a year, you may want to increase your contribution to the maximum rate your employer allows so you can put away as much as you can afford while you're still part of a plan.

In December, you might want to change your rate to bring your contribution to the full amount you can contribute for the year. If that's the case, don't wait until the Friday after Thanksgiving to tell your 401(k) administrator. It may be too late.

What's Yours Is Yours, But…

All contributions to your 401(k) aren't created equal.

Because the money that you put into your 401(k) is part of your salary, it's yours from the day it goes into your account. So are any earnings your contributions produce, and any amounts that you've rolled into your current plan from a previous employer's plan. If you leave your job for any reason, you usually have the right to decide what happens to those assets.

In contrast, in most cases you have to earn any matching contribution your employer makes and earnings those contributions produce by working long enough at the job to **vest**, or have a legal right to that money. If you leave before the required vesting period is up, you forfeit some or all of that portion of your account.

The time required for vesting isn't arbitrary. It's a matter of federal law. You must be fully vested either after five years of service or at least 20% vested after three years and fully vested after seven.

COUNTING THE DAYS

A year may be 365 days to you, but the government doesn't want there to be any question about what counts as a year of service. So your employer can count your time on the job in one of two ways:

1 Using the annual, or elapsed time, method, your employer counts each 12-month period from the day you're hired to the anniversary of that day as one year. If you were hired on July 10, 1995, and you left the company on July 8, 2000, you would have been on the job for only four years since you didn't complete five full 12-month cycles.

2 Using the hourly method, each 1,000 hours you work within a 12-month period counts as a year of service. So if you worked 40 hours a week for 25 weeks, you'd be credited as having been on the job for a year. As a result, you might qualify to join the plan before you'd been on the job a full calendar year. After your first year, which begins the day

Hourly

Making the Grade

Some employers provide **immediate vesting** as a job benefit. Others offer **cliff** or **graded vesting**. Graded vesting gives you the right to an increasing percentage of their contribution over a fixed period.

For example, in a four-year graded plan, you may be 25% vested in the first year, 50% in the second year, and by the end of the fourth year, you're 100% vested. In a five-year graded plan, you are vested 20% in the first year, and so on, until the end of the fifth year, when you are fully vested.

Some employers prefer cliff vesting, an all-or-nothing approach. With three-year cliff vesting, you would be 100% vested after three years. But if you left the job after two years and 11 months, you'd walk off the cliff, forfeiting all of your employer's contributions and any earnings that portion of your account may have produced.

While your employer's contributions may not be worth sticking around for if you get a better job offer, it's smart to check out how much you'd be giving up if you left shortly before a vesting date.

For example, if your employer matched 50% of your contribution in

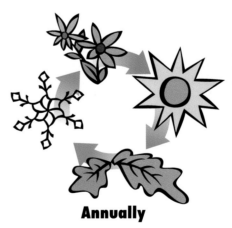

Annually

you start your job, your employer has some flexibility in setting the date at which a 12-month period begins.

Your employer may actually use both the annual and hourly methods, applying one to establish your eligibility for the plan, and the other to determine when you're vested. Vesting rules, like all 401(k) rules, have to be the same for all employees.

or Scaling the Cliff

each of four years, that could easily amount to $10,000 or more if you'd been putting away the maximum each year.

Waiting until you vested after five years could be enough of an incentive to postpone a move.

There are three types of vesting schedules

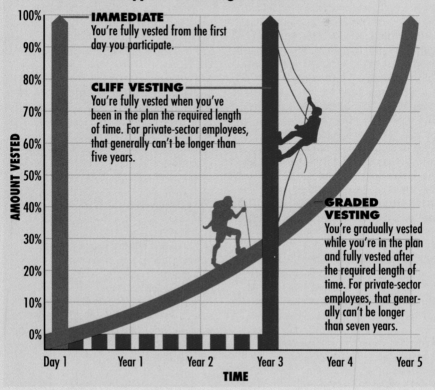

IMMEDIATE
You're fully vested from the first day you participate.

CLIFF VESTING
You're fully vested when you've been in the plan the required length of time. For private-sector employees, that generally can't be longer than five years.

GRADED VESTING
You're gradually vested while you're in the plan and fully vested after the required length of time. For private-sector employees, that generally can't be longer than seven years.

AMOUNT VESTED: 100%, 90%, 80%, 70%, 60%, 50%, 40%, 30%, 20%, 10%, 0%

TIME: Day 1, Year 1, Year 2, Year 3, Year 4, Year 5

INSTANT VESTING

A few exceptions to the vesting rules give you ownership of the full value of your account before you'd otherwise be entitled to it. You become fully vested, regardless of the number of years you've spent on your job, if:

- Your employer ends the company's plan
- Your employer fires more than 20% of the workforce at one time
- You're officially disabled and can no longer work
- You turn 65 while working

FEEDING THE KITTY

The employer contributions you leave behind at your old job before you're vested go back to your employer. They can be distributed among the other employees in the 401(k) plan or used to offset future employer contributions.

BACK TO WORK

All may not be lost if you leave a job before you're fully vested. If you're part of a 401(k) plan when you leave, and you end up going back to work for the same employer, the years you worked before you left still count toward your vesting period.

If you weren't part of the plan then, but want to join it when you rejoin the company, your prior years of service may or may not count. It usually depends on how long you worked at the company the first time, and how long you've been away. But don't hesitate to ask your plan manager about what your plan provides.

Additional Contributions

How full do you want to fill your 401(k)?

An **aftertax contribution** is money you put into your 401(k) over and above the amount of pretax salary you can contribute each year. The most you can add is the difference between the government's limit for the year and your employer's ceiling on contributions, which is usually 10% or 15% of your salary.

For example, if your salary is $100,000, a 15% contribution would be $15,000. With a cap of $10,500, you could add up to $4,500 to make up the difference.

Your employer might even match some of what you add, although that tends to be a less common practice than matching pretax contributions. The key benefit of making aftertax contributions is the potential to produce an even larger retirement income because earnings may accumulate on a larger base.

WITHDRAWAL ISSUES

Unlike pretax contributions, which are subject to income tax and an early withdrawal penalty if you take them out of your 401(k) account before you reach 59½, you can withdraw aftertax contributions from most plans at any time. But the rules are complicated, so you'll want to check with your tax adviser about the consequences of taking a withdrawal.

Here's a simplified summary: You owe no income tax and no early withdrawal penalty on your contribution. But you'll have to pay income tax on any investment gains or income, such as interest or dividends. You'll also owe the 10% early withdrawal penalty on the earnings.

You can't get around this problem by withdrawing just principal—except on contributions made before 1986 when the law governing withdrawals changed. If you want to take out aftertax contributions made in 1987 or later, you have to withdraw equal proportions of principal and earnings, which may mean you'll owe a penalty on more than half of what you take out.

But if you really need access to your aftertax contributions, you may have an option. Under some plans, you can withdraw those amounts and any earnings they have produced and roll over just the earnings portion into an individual retirement account (IRA), to avoid taxes and penalties. Not all plans offer this option, though, so be sure to check with your plan administrator.

YOU WANT TO TAKE THE PLUNGE

Putting extra money into a 401(k) account can sometimes be a good strategy. You may want to consider it if:

- You're eligible to receive a company match on aftertax contributions and don't want to pass up free money
- You've already contributed to a Roth IRA but still have aftertax money to invest
- You don't qualify for a Roth because your income is too high
- You have good investment choices and pay minimal fees with your employer's plan

BUT TEST THE WATERS FIRST

Putting aftertax money into your 401(k) can help build your account value by providing a larger base on which earnings can accumulate tax-deferred. But before you make these additions to your account, keep in mind that:

- Putting in extra money won't reduce the portion of your salary that's taxable
- Rolling over your 401(k) into an IRA will be more complicated
- Rolling over your 401(k) into a new employer's plan may not be possible
- Figuring the tax you owe on withdrawals will be more complicated

INCOME

IN EXCESS

What you don't want to do is make an excess contribution, which means adding pretax income above the government cap. That might happen, for example, if you got a raise and forgot to lower your contribution rate. Unless you take the money out before the end of the year, you'll owe a 10% penalty for each year it's in your account.

Pretax Contribution

You make pretax contributions, sometimes called elective contributions or elective deferrals, by reducing or deferring your salary. That means you postpone income tax on the contribution and on the earnings the contribution may provide until you withdraw them from the plan.

You make aftertax contributions from income you receive and pay tax on. But any earnings are tax deferred until you withdraw them.

Aftertax Contribution

Total 401(k) Contribution

IRA ALTERNATIVES

If you qualify to make a full $2,000 contribution to a Roth IRA because you have an adjusted gross income of $95,000 if you're single, or $150,000 if you're married and file a joint return, you may be better off putting money into the IRA than making additional contributions to a 401(k).

You'll have more control over how the money is invested, and after you turn 59½, you can withdraw tax-free earnings, provided your account has been open at least five years. While the $2,000 you can put into a Roth is less than you might be able to add to your 401(k), you'll avoid a lot of complexity (and income taxes) when you do withdraw.

If you're looking for other tax-deferred options for investing outside of your 401(k), you may want to consider traditional IRAs and variable annuities. With each type of investment, you're contributing aftertax income and will owe tax at your regular rates when you withdraw any earnings from your account. And, in most cases, you'll also have to pay a 10% penalty if you withdraw from either type of account before you reach 59½. But there may be exceptions to the penalty if you're withdrawing money to pay college expenses, buy a first home, cover medical bills, or if you die or are disabled.

You might want to put money into an IRA first and then consider an annuity, or simply go straight to the annuity. There are no contribution limits on annuities, but they carry some expenses that IRAs don't. Here are some of the things you should consider:

- The amount you' ll have to contribute
- The control you'll have over how the money is invested
- The fees you'll pay
- The withdrawal requirements and penalties
- The payout options

Naming a Beneficiary

You want a beneficiary who's right for the part.

Since you put money into a 401(k) plan to provide the retirement income you may need, it may seem strange that one of your first major decisions is to determine your **beneficiary**—the person, people, or institution you designate to get what's left in your account when you die. But the choice is an important one, both for you and for your beneficiary.

WHAT'S AT STAKE

If you participate in a retirement savings plan for most of the years you work, you may well accumulate a substantial amount of money. Once you retire, you might make large withdrawals in the early years if your plan allows them, or you might live a long time and use up most of the account value during your lifetime.

But there's always the possibility of dying before you've spent all the money in your account, or even before you've begun to withdraw it at all. That's one

reason that designating a beneficiary is so important—so the people you care about get to benefit from the money that's left.

For example, you might feel strongly about providing income for your spouse, child, grandchild, or other family member. Or, you might want that money to go to a close friend, or to a favorite charity. But if you don't officially name a beneficiary, the chances are that the people you want to receive the money won't. What's more, you run the very real risk that more income tax will be due more quickly than if you'd named a beneficiary who could withdraw from the account over a period of time.

DIRECT BENEFITS

It's important to keep in mind that retirement plan assets are different from other types of property—such as investments in taxable accounts or real estate—which you can pass to your heirs by naming them in your will or making gifts while you're alive. In fact, retirement savings plans work more like life insurance policies. If your policy is in effect when you die, the **death benefit**—also known as the face value—is paid directly to the person you've identified as beneficiary.

Similarly, at your death, assets remaining in your 401(k) pass directly to the beneficiary you've named or to a trust that benefits that person. What's different about a 401(k) is that your beneficiary should be able to collect income from your plan over an extended period of time instead of all at once as is typical of insurance policies.

DIRECTOR

DOING THE DEED

When you join a 401(k) plan the enrollment form usually requests—even requires—that you designate a beneficiary. In fact, your plan administrator may return your application as incomplete if you've left the beneficiary section blank.

If your choice is straightforward—for example, naming your spouse and your children if your spouse dies before you do—then completing any standard form is all that's needed.

If your choice is more complicated, such as naming both a person and a charity to share the benefit, you need to check your plan's provisions. You'll probably want to consult an attorney who specializes in retirement or estate planning. That adviser can create a form that's compatible with what your plan allows, so you can make the designation you prefer. But experts caution that you shouldn't try to create such a document on your own. The laws are complex and the potential tax implications are huge.

ANOTHER CONSIDERATION
Since beneficiary designations, including those for a 401(k), are never public information as the provisions of a will are, you may think that your designation is a private matter. But designations can be challenged, just as wills can be.

PRIVATE
Beneficiary designation

CONTINUING TAX BREAKS

If your plan permits installment payments, even as your beneficiary receives income from the account, the remaining balance may continue to grow tax-deferred. That can help to provide even more income over a longer period of time—recognizing, of course, that investment growth is not guaranteed.

What's more, the tax due on income from a 401(k) is also spread out over the entire period that distributions are made, posing little risk of bumping your beneficiary's income into a higher tax bracket. Although your beneficiary pays taxes on this income at his or her regular tax rate rather than at the lower capital gains rate that applies to some inherited assets, the steady income may be very welcome.

Despite these income and tax advantages to your beneficiaries, it's probably not wise to think of your 401(k) primarily as an estate-building tool. That's because once you reach age 70½, you'll have to begin taking money from the account whether you need the income or not. And if you live long enough, there may be very little left to pass on.

The switch to beneficiary distribution

YOU

YOUR BENEFICIARY

Value

YOUR 401(k)

Time

SECOND GUESSING
If you don't name a beneficiary when you enroll in a 401(k) plan, the plan administrator may designate your spouse—if you're married—and probably your estate if you're not. It pays to check whether that's the case with your plan.

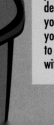

BENEFITS TO YOU

While it's important to name a beneficiary for your 401(k) plan to provide the greatest possible legacy with the fewest possible tax consequences, there's another reason to think carefully about your decision. The beneficiary you name can make a substantial difference in the amount you must withdraw from your account each year once you reach 70½ and begin taking required distributions.

An Investment Menu

Most 401(k) plans offer a good choice of investments.

Potentially the most rewarding—but also most intimidating—part of managing your 401(k) plan is deciding how to invest the money you're putting into your account. That's because your investment selections make a major difference in how quickly your contribution may increase in value, and the income your plan will provide after you retire.

IT'S ALL IN THE MIX

Experts agree that, regardless of the number of options a plan offers, it should have a diversified mix. For example, a plan offering only mutual funds might provide an adequate mix if it includes choices in each of these categories:

- Stock mutual funds that specialize in large-company, midsized-company, small-company, and international stock
- Bond mutual funds that specialize in long-term corporate and long-term government bonds
- Balanced funds, which buy both stocks and bonds
- Money market funds

Some plans also offer a set of **lifecycle funds**. You can think of a lifecycle fund as a package of stock and bond funds that have been selected as likely to provide a particular level of investment return, from conservative to potentially quite aggressive. You choose one lifecycle fund in the set as appropriate to your investment objectives, and the fund manager distributes your contributions among the individual funds that are included in that package. You don't have to make any additional choices to get the balance you seek.

MENU OFFERINGS MAY VARY

Most 401(k) plans let you choose among at least three investments, and many plans offer more—a dozen or more mutual funds, for example, as well as selections in other categories.

A plan sponsor, or employer, who provides a minimum of three distinctly different investments—which means that each of them puts money to work in a way different from the others and exposes you to a different level of risk—is following voluntary guidelines set by the US Department of Labor. One of the government's goals in establishing those guidelines is to ensure that as you and other employees take on more responsibility for providing your own retirement income, you have real choices about the investments you make.

Offering a range of choices is also good for employers who, as plan **fiduciaries**, are legally responsible for selecting a plan's investment options to serve the participants' best interest. They are also

THE LIMITS OF CHOICE

Every 401(k) plan lets you decide how to invest the contributions you make from among the plan's offerings. Some plans also let you decide how to invest any contributions your employer makes. Other plans let your employer decide how to direct any matching contributions, which includes the right to invest the match in company stock.

If your plan doesn't match your contributions, or it provides limited investment choices, you may be better off contributing less than the maximum to your account. Instead, you might want to consider putting up to $2,000 of the money you would have deposited in your 401(k) into a traditional or Roth IRA, where you have more flexibility to invest as you choose.

A SHOPPING LIST

The average 401(k) plan offers eight to ten investment choices, typically a combination of:
- Mutual funds
- Guaranteed investment contracts (GICs)
- Company stock
- Variable annuities

But as the number of employees who participate in 401(k) plans grows, and as participants develop investing experience, the demand for more and better choices escalates. In response, many employers are adding alternatives, mostly mutual funds, to their investment menus. A few companies have expanded the number of plan choices to 100 or more. Others provide access to brokerage accounts, called **windows**, through which employees can purchase individual stocks and bonds as well as mutual funds.

responsible for monitoring investment performance. By complying with government guidelines, employers are protected against lawsuits charging that they're liable for your investment losses— or the losses of any other employee participating in the plan.

In other words, by giving you enough investment choices, employers limit their legal liability. If investments you choose don't perform as well as expected, the responsibility is yours since you could have made other choices.

IS MORE BETTER?

Experts disagree about whether it's an advantage to have a long list of investment options. Some believe that the more choices you have, the better. That's based on the conviction that variety gives you more control over the level of investment return you can realize.

But others argue that having too many choices is not only confusing but potentially self-defeating. They say that too much choice even discourages participation by making the selection process too complex. They fear employees may just throw up their hands in frustration and use the dartboard approach to investing, or some other equally arbitrary method. Or worse yet, they worry that employees may not participate at all.

DOES YOUR PLAN MEASURE UP?

Of course, no plan is perfect. While most administrators try to provide a broad range of well-chosen investments, some plans are cobbled together from randomly selected lists of funds or other retirement savings products available from a bank, insurance company, or mutual fund company that offers your employer a good deal for administering the plan.

If your plan's options seem unsatisfactory because they're too limited, or because the selections are uneven, you may want to invest just enough to qualify for a company match, and put the rest of your retirement assets elsewhere.

Or you might try to mobilize fellow employees to request a better group of choices. It's a goal that people at all levels of the organization should be able to agree on, since everyone will benefit.

Mutual Funds

Mutual funds provide the muscle for most 401(k) plans.

It's no coincidence that mutual funds are the most common 401(k) investments, or that the expanding number of mutual funds in recent years parallels increasing participation in 401(k) plans. In many ways, the two are a perfect match.

Mutual funds are liquid investments, issuing shares as investors want to buy them and redeeming shares as investors want to sell. So they're set up to handle regular purchases, such as the amount you contribute to your plan each pay period. Every time money goes into your account, you buy as many whole and fractional shares as your contribution will pay for.

Mutual funds are also good choices for 401(k) plans because they're diversified. That means that even small amounts of money invested in one mutual fund can help protect you from the investment risk that you would face in owning stock in just one company or buying a single bond. And

MUTUAL FUND PRICE TAGS

What you pay to buy a mutual fund share depends on the fund's **net asset value (NAV)** plus any **load**, or sales charge that the fund charges at the time of purchase.

A fund's NAV, or the dollar value of a single share, is calculated by dividing the total value of the fund's assets, known as its **underlying investments**, by the number of existing shares. It's figured at the close of every trading day. For example, a fund with underlying assets of $200 million and 10 million existing shares would have a NAV of $20.

For a no-load fund, which has no sales charge, or class B or class C shares, whose sales charges don't apply when you buy, you pay the NAV. For the funds that charge a load when you buy, which are known as Class A shares, you pay the **maximum offering price (MOP)**, which is the NAV plus the sales charge.

Expert management   **Redeemability**   **Diversification**   **Lower trading costs**

because there's a wide variety of funds investing in different markets, you can continue to diversify as you add funds to your portfolio.

Because mutual funds are managed investments, buy and sell decisions are made by an experienced professional who has access to market research and analysis. While that doesn't guarantee you'll get the returns you'd like, it means you don't have to make your own trading decisions. And because mutual fund managers invest such large amounts of money, their trading costs are lower than yours would be if you bought and sold investments on your own. The funds pass that cost saving along to you.

TO TURN OR NOT TO TURN

The rate at which a fund buys and sells investments, or its **turnover rate**, may be something to consider when you choose funds. That's because the costs of constant buying and selling can reduce the return a fund provides. On the other hand, some funds with high turnover rates produce stellar returns because they earn significant profits on their transactions.

AN INSIDE VIEW

Unlike real estate, which has a physical presence, or a share of stock, which represents a sliver of ownership in a corpoation, a mutual fund is best defined by what it does.

A mutual fund buys and sells stocks, bonds, or other securities. The money that the fund manager uses to make these purchases comes from you and other investors, some of them individuals and some of them institutions, including 401(k)s and other retirement plans, who buy shares in the fund.

A mutual fund makes money two ways: by earning dividends or interest on the investments it owns and by selling investments that have gone up in price, producing capital gains. It **distributes**, or pays out, its earnings and capital gains (minus fees and expenses) to you and its other investors. In a 401(k) plan, of course, those distributions are automatically reinvested in the fund to increase the number of shares you own.

Some funds buy and sell investments regularly, while others hold certain investments for long periods of time. Most decisions to sell or hold depend on the goals the manager is trying to achieve and his or her investment style. But sell decisions may also be driven by the fund's obligation to redeem shares that investors want to sell.

FUND CREATION

When a new fund is created, an investment company—sometimes a company that sells only mutual funds, and sometimes a bank or other financial institution—develops its idea for the fund, prepares marketing materials, sells the shares, hires the fund manager or managers, and oversees the fund's operations.

In most cases, in fact, a company offers several different funds, each developed to meet a different investment objective, appeal to different investors, or to respond to changes in the financial markets.

How Distribution Works

401(k) MUTUAL FUND

Dividends and capital gains are reinvested

BLOOD RELATIONS

Collectively, an investment company's funds are known as a **family of funds**. Like flesh-and-blood families, some groups of funds are more extensive than others, and some seem to be more successful.

You may discover that all of the funds offered through your 401(k) plan are members of a single family. That's most likely to be the case when the plan is managed by an investment company or financial institution offering its own funds.

That's not necessarily a bad thing. But you should recognize that simply being a member of such a family doesn't mean each fund is an equally appropriate investment for a 401(k) or that it may provide the return you're looking for. You have to evaluate each fund separately, choosing only those that meet your requirements.

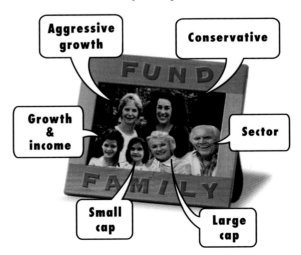

Aggressive growth

Conservative

Growth & income

Sector

FUND

Small cap

Large cap

FAMILY

Fund Facts

Funds have many similarities but also major differences.

Mutual funds fall into three broad categories, sometimes called **asset classes**. They differ from each other most significantly in the kinds of investments they make:

- Stock mutual funds buy shares of stock in publicly traded corporations
- Bond mutual funds buy bonds issued by public corporations, by federal, state, and local governments, and by public agencies
- Money market funds buy a variety of short-term investments from various sources

All funds, regardless of category, have some important similarities. For example, they all take in and invest pools of money, collect earnings on their investments, and distribute those earnings to their shareholders. And they all allow you to reinvest your earnings to buy additional shares.

But the categories, and the funds within these categories, also have some important differences. To begin with, each asset class puts your money to work to produce a different result: stock funds to provide growth in value, bond funds to provide a source of income, and money market funds to keep your capital intact. And each fund within each category has a clearly defined approach to reaching the broad goal of the group to which it belongs. That goal is called its **investment objective**.

THE SHARE QUESTION

Although you buy shares in a mutual fund, which makes you a part owner of the fund's assets, it's not the same as buying shares in a public corporation. When a corporation sells stock, it issues a specific number of shares. Once they're in the marketplace, those shares change hands among investors, sometimes rapidly and sometimes more slowly as demand for them changes. But the corporation itself is out of the trading loop unless it buys back shares to reduce the number in the open market, or it increases the number by splitting existing ones or issuing additional shares.

A mutual fund issues shares as investors want to buy them and redeems shares as investors want to sell, so that the number changes all the time. The price per share is based on the value of the underlying investments and the number of shares, not on what you or anyone else will pay to own a share of the fund.

FINDING FUND INFORMATION

When you get the list of the funds your 401(k) plan offers, you need to investigate their investment objectives, management styles, levels of risk, and fees before you select those that will work best for you. Check each fund's prospectus, a document that provides all the information you're looking for. The prospectus also includes financial reports, a list of the actual investments the fund holds, and other details.

If your plan offers **retail funds**, also called brand-name funds, which are those available to investors on their own as well as to plan participants, you can check what independent analysts at Lipper Inc., Morningstar, Inc., and Value Line, Inc. have to say about them. See if your library subscribes to these reports or ask your financial adviser for copies. You can also look for coverage of these funds in the financial press.

If your plan offers **institutional funds**, which are created for the financial institution that provides your plan, and aren't available in the retail market, you'll have to get information about these funds directly from the provider.

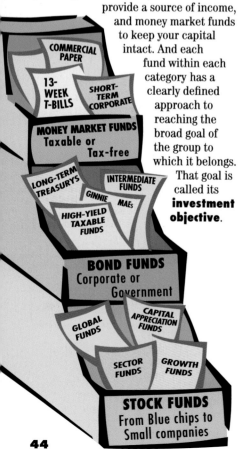

COMMERCIAL PAPER

13-WEEK T-BILLS

SHORT-TERM CORPORATE

MONEY MARKET FUNDS
Taxable or Tax-free

LONG-TERM TREASURYS

INTERMEDIATE FUNDS

GINNIE MAEs

HIGH-YIELD TAXABLE FUNDS

BOND FUNDS
Corporate or Government

GLOBAL FUNDS

CAPITAL APPRECIATION FUNDS

SECTOR FUNDS

GROWTH FUNDS

STOCK FUNDS
From Blue chips to Small companies

MANAGER'S SPECIAL

Another way mutual funds differ from one another is in their management **style**, or the approach a portfolio manager uses to choose the fund's investments.

Two stock funds that share an investment objective—say, providing long-term increase in value—might own portfolios that are very much alike or that are strikingly different. In the first instance, they might both focus on stock in up-and-coming new companies, or companies on the cutting edge of new technologies. Or, a fund with a more growth-oriented manager

might emphasize new-company stocks while the other, with a value-oriented manager, might buy stocks of well-known companies whose sales prices are in a slump, but that the manager expects to rebound.

Both of these funds might provide strong returns over an extended period of time. But their returns would probably be significantly different in the short term, since growth stocks tend to prosper in a different set of economic circumstances than value stocks.

CONTRARIAN *Invest in what others avoid*

Being Objective

When a mutual fund defines its financial goal, it's identifying a specific set of investments—though not individual investments—that will be the core of its portfolio. That set is a segment of the broader asset class to which the fund belongs.

For example, if a stock fund describes its objective as a combination of steady growth in value and current income, it is saying that it will concentrate on stock in large, financially sound companies that pay regular dividends. That doesn't mean the fund won't buy some stock in companies that don't fit that mold precisely. But it does mean the manager is unlikely to buy stock in start-up companies that pay no dividends at all.

The relationship between objective and type of investment is based on the way various types of investments have performed over time. In this example, stock in a large company that pays dividends typically increases in value more slowly than stock in a successful new company, but tends to pay its dividends regularly.

There's no fixed number of investment objectives, and the differences between similar sounding objectives aren't always that clear. In addition, the relationship between a fund's stated objective and its current performance isn't always precise. But those cautions aside, looking at a fund's investment objective is a good place to start when you're selecting possible 401(k) investments. What you're looking for are funds whose objectives match your own.

MUTUAL FUND GOAL

FUND MANAGEMENT

Stock Funds

Stock funds are the stars in the mutual fund universe.

It's no accident that most of the funds offered in a typical 401(k) plan are stock funds. There are more stock funds, and more varieties of them, than any other type of fund. In fact, more than 75% of 401(k) assets nationwide are invested in stock funds.

There are reasons for all that popularity. Because their underlying investments are stocks in publicly traded companies, which as a group have historically outperformed other types of investments, stock funds have also provided stronger investment returns than other types of funds. And it's strong returns that make your 401(k) account worth more as time goes by.

THE FUND AS INVESTOR

A stock fund buys in much bigger quantities than you and other individuals do, and typically buys and sells at a faster pace. But it chooses its investments for the same reasons:

- Most funds choose stocks so they can make money by selling at a higher price than they paid
- Some funds choose stocks to earn dividends that the corporation pays its stockholders

RELATIVES...NOT CLONES

Stock funds are designed to suit different investment goals. Some make relatively conservative investments by concentrating on well-established companies sometimes described as **blue chips**. Their goal is steady if sometimes modest growth in value, dividend payments that can be reinvested, and limited risk from major losses resulting from business failure or volatile stock prices. These funds may have names like Blue Chip, Growth and Income, Dividend Growth, or sometimes Large-cap Growth.

At the other end of the spectrum, some stock funds, with names like Aggressive Growth, Capital Appreciation, or almost any word combined with New or

MATTERS OF SIZE

Stock funds are sometimes identified as large-cap, mid-cap, or small-cap. That's because funds are designed to invest in companies of different sizes, identified by their **market capitalizations**, or market caps. Large-cap companies have market caps over $5 billion. Mid-cap companies have caps over $1.5 billion but less than $5 billion, and small-caps are companies whose market capitalization is less than $1.5 billion. You figure a company's market cap by multiplying the current price of its stock by the number of existing shares.

Price per share
x Number of shares
= Company cap

Large-cap company Over $5 billion

Mid-cap company $1.5–$5 billion

Small-cap company <$1.5 billion

MUTUAL FUNDS

LARGE CAP

STOCK

STOCK

AGGRESSIVE GROWTH

STOCK

STOCK

Discovery, tend to invest in younger companies that managers believe have the potential to be much more valuable in the future than they are today. Because they're often start-ups or cutting-edge companies, there's also a significant risk that some of them may fail, which puts some of your capital at risk.

Between these extremes are thousands of other funds, some investing in a broad range of companies and others more narrowly focused on stocks in a single industry or sector.

Market cap makes a difference in the way a fund's underlying investments can be expected to perform, which has a direct impact on the performance of the fund itself. Generally, the smaller the average market capitalization of the companies in a fund, the more volatile the stock price. So when you invest in a small-cap fund, you can expect greater risk but also the potential for greater reward.

That's because the smaller the company, the fewer financial reserves it's likely to have to carry it through a period of economic slowdown. As you might expect, the opposite is true of large-caps. They're generally thought of as more stable and less risky.

Technology companies and the funds that invest in them may be exceptions. They can be some of the biggest companies in the world, measured by market capitalization. But their prices still tend to be extremely volatile. So a large-cap fund with major investments in Internet companies might behave more like a small-cap fund than a large-cap fund investing in blue chip companies.

Stock funds are also known as equity funds. Equity means ownership, and when a fund buys shares of stock it is buying partial ownership of the corporation issuing the stock.

NARROW SLICES

Many stock fund portfolios include 100 or more companies whose products and services span many different parts of the economy. For example, a typical fund might own stock in companies whose businesses are as varied as electronics, automobiles, retail clothing, financial services, software, pharmaceuticals, energy, technology, and telecommunications. In fact, diversified portfolios of this kind are one of the defining features of mutual funds. And investors consider diversification one of their greatest appeals.

Another breed, called **sector funds**, invests only in the stocks of a particular segment of the economy or in a particular industry, such as energy or telecommunications. Because of their specialization, these funds are out of step with the underlying principle of diversification. While a sector fund is more diversified than a single stock, since it might own dozens of stocks in its area of interest, there's nothing in the fund's portfolio that could offset a downturn in the sector it invests in.

Since any sector can be highly volatile, these funds provide an opportunity for big profits if you're invested at the right time. But there is always the equal and opposite risk that one year's strong sector may provide weak returns the next.

Bond Funds

Bond funds are hybrid investments: part equity and part debt.

When you put money into a bond fund, you buy shares in the fund, just as you do when you put money into a stock fund. The fund manager invests that money by buying bonds issued by corporations, governments, or government agencies.

When issuers sell bonds, they're actually borrowing money from investors—in this case, bond funds—who are willing to lend for a specific period of time, called the bond's **term**. In exchange, the fund receives interest on the loan and the promise that the **principal**, or loan amount, will be returned by a specific date, called the **maturity date**.

Since the issuer owes the investors money, bonds are also called **debt securities**. It's a way to distinguish them from equity securities, or stocks, which give investors partial ownership.

How Bonds Work in Your 401(k)

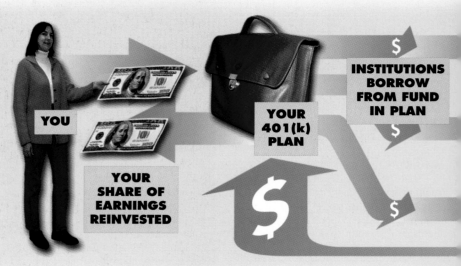

YOU

YOUR SHARE OF EARNINGS REINVESTED

YOUR 401(k) PLAN

INSTITUTIONS BORROW FROM FUND IN PLAN

BOND FUND-AMENTALS

You differentiate bond funds from each other in two ways: by the type of issuer and by the average term of the bonds in the fund. 401(k) plans generally offer four categories of bond funds:

- US Treasury funds, which invest in bills, notes, or bonds issued by the federal government
- Agency funds, which invest in bonds issued by agencies that are part of or affiliated with the federal government
- US corporate funds, which invest in bonds issued by US companies of various sizes
- International funds, which invest in bonds issued by corporations based overseas or by governments other than the US

Funds may focus on bonds of different terms, grouped by average maturities:

- Short-term funds, which have an average maturity of one to three years
- Intermediate-term funds, which have an average maturity of three to ten years
- Long-term funds, which have an average maturity of 10 years or longer

COMPLEX INTEREST

In most cases, if you own an individual bond, the rate of interest you earn remains the same for the term of the loan. But that's not the case with a bond fund.

While each bond that a fund owns pays a fixed rate of interest, every bond in the fund—and there may be dozens—is likely to be paying at a different rate. In addition, the fund's portfolio of bonds is always in flux, so that the collective rate the fund earns on one day may not be the same as its collective rate the next day.

CHANGING INTEREST, CHANGING FUND PRICES

As interest rates change in the economy at large—going higher in some periods and dropping in others, often in response to policy decisions by the Federal Reserve Bank—the interest rates a bond fund earns and the distributions it makes to its shareholders reflect these changes.

Fluctuating interest rates also affect a bond fund's **net asset value (NAV)**, or price per share. When rates drop, the share price of a bond fund increases because the bonds it owns, which pay a higher rate of interest than new issues in the market, increase in value. The reverse is also true. When rates rise, share prices of bond funds drop because newly issued bonds pay a higher rate than the bonds the fund owns.

As a bond fund's NAV changes in response to changes in the interest rates, the market value of your holding in the fund changes as well. In a simplified example, if you bought 100 shares with a NAV of $10 , your account value would be $1,000. But if the NAV dropped to $9.75 because of rising interest rates, your account value would be $975. That's an example of interest rate risk.

In addition, the value of a bond also changes based on supply and demand. An existing bond is worth more when rates drop because investors will pay more than its **par value**, or price at issue, to own it, so they can earn the higher interest rate it will pay. And they'll pay less for existing bonds when rates rise because they can earn better rates on newer ones.

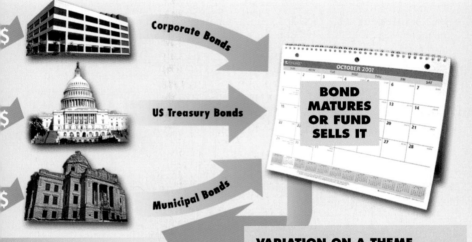

BOND MATURES OR FUND SELLS IT

Corporate Bonds

US Treasury Bonds

Municipal Bonds

PRICE AND YIELD

Yield is a measure of what you earn on a bond fund. When you own an individual bond for its full term, your yield is the same as the interest rate the bond pays. But when you own a bond fund, your yield changes as the fund's NAV changes. The yield drops as the NAV rises, and rises as the NAV drops.

If NAV rises Yield drops   If NAV drops Yield rises

TRACKING TOTAL RETURN

From an investment perspective, what matters most about owning shares in a bond fund is **total return**—the interest you earn plus any increase or decrease in the value of your principal. The greater

VARIATION ON A THEME

Bonds are often described as fixed-income investments. That's because most bonds pay a fixed rate of interest on a fixed schedule. But it's not really accurate to describe a bond fund as a fixed-income investment, since the interest rate you earn varies from payment to payment as the fund's portfolio of bonds changes.

your total return, the better your investment is doing. The longer a bond fund's average maturity, the more sensitive it is to changes in interest rates. Thus, a long-term bond fund has greater potential than a short-term bond fund to generate high total returns when rates are declining, and low total returns when rates are rising.

Higher-yielding issues, sometimes known as **junk bond funds**, or more politely as **high-yield funds**, are generally the most volatile. The interest rate they offer is high, which can boost total return, but their underlying investment can decline precipitously in value.

Capital Preservation

Investing too conservatively may not be as smart as it seems.

Stable value funds and guaranteed income contracts (GICs) are designed to preserve capital, which means reducing the risk that your investment will lose money. For example, if you put $10,000 into a capital preservation fund, you should reasonably expect that the value of that fund will never be less than $10,000. The downside is that a capital preservation account is less likely to provide long-term protection against inflation.

STABLE VALUE FUNDS

A stable value fund guarantees the value of your initial investment, or **principal**, and promises a fixed rate of return.

A stable value fund may buy US Treasury and corporate bonds as well as interest-bearing contracts from banks and insurance companies. Or all of the fund's assets may go into GICs.

The sponsor, typically an insurance company, establishes the value of the fixed-income investments at the time of purchase, arriving at what's known as book value. After valuation, the net asset value of the fund and the price of each share remain constant, unrelated to the changing market value of the fund's holdings.

Stable value funds pay interest at a higher rate than money market mutual funds, providing a stronger hedge against inflation. That's because the fund's investments have longer maturity dates than the investments made by money market funds, and pay higher interest. The higher rates are one reason some experts recommend stable value funds for investors who want to diversify a 401(k) account that contains more volatile investments, such as stock mutual funds or bond mutual funds.

However, the interest rate on a stable value fund is generally guaranteed for only a predetermined time, sometimes as brief as three months, and varies with changing market conditions. In some plans, you may have to pay a fee, sometimes a substantial one, for shifting money out of a stable value account.

GUARANTEED INVESTMENT CONTRACTS (GICs)

Investors concerned about losing their principal by buying securities that they consider too risky may choose to put some of their retirement plan savings into guaranteed investment contracts (GICs).

These contracts are insurance company products that resemble individual bonds (not bond funds) or bank certificates of deposit (CDs). The issuer has the use of your money for the term of the contract, and pays a fixed rate of interest in return. At the end of the specified term, often one year but sometimes as long as five years, you get back your principal plus interest. You can use that lump sum to buy another contract paying the current interest rate or invest your money elsewhere.

NIBBLING AT YOUR ACCOUNT

While GICs are often described as safe investments, they actually pose a number of risks. The major problem is that the return on a GIC is unlikely to outpace inflation over the long term, leaving you short of the income you need in retirement.

WHAT'S IN A NAME?

Though the name suggests that a stable value fund is a mutual fund, that's not actually the case. A more accurate parallel is to unit investment trusts (UITs).

In addition, you can face substantial penalties for switching money out of a GIC, including forfeiting a percentage of your principal. That's because GIC assets are themselves invested in fixed income investments that provide a higher rate of return than the insurer guarantees you. If the insurer has to sell those investments to redeem your principal, it puts the insurer's profit at risk—a loss that's passed along to you.

You should also be aware that if you put money in a GIC and the insurer goes out of business, you may receive a lower interest rate than you were promised. And it may also take longer than expected to get your principal back.

However, you can evaluate the issuer's economic strength and its ability to meet its obligations by checking the company's credit rating before you purchase a GIC. Those ratings are available online from Standard & Poor's (www.standardand poor.com), Moody's Investor Services (www.moodys.com), and A.M. Best and Company (www.ambest.com). You can also ask your plan administrator for this information.

MONEY MARKET FUNDS

Money market funds are also designed to preserve principal by investing in cash equivalents, or short-term debts of corpo-rations, banks, and the US government. These funds try to keep the value of each share at $1. For example, a money market fund might buy 13-week US Treasury bills or **commercial paper**, which is a corpo-rate loan with a maturity as short as a few days or as long as a few months. Since the terms are short, there's little danger that interest rates will change significantly. And since most of the issuers have high credit ratings, there's very little chance of default.

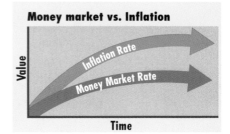

Money market vs. Inflation

PROS AND CONS OF MONEY MARKET FUNDS

Money market funds have their good points. You earn interest, typically at a slightly higher rate than you would get on an insured bank account. And, you can usually move money in and out of the fund without penalty or loss of value.

On the other hand, since that interest rate is unlikely to be significantly greater than the rate of inflation, you won't earn enough over time to keep up with the in-creasing cost of living.

When you own a money market fund outside a 401(k), it can play an impor-tant role in managing your money, since you can use it as a parking place for cash you're planning to invest elsewhere. But since you can allo-cate your 401(k) contributions to various investments as you add money to your account, a money market fund may serve little purpose dur-ing the time you're build-ing your account.

Growth

The Risk of Inflation

Depletion
40/01

More Fund Choices

You might put your money on a horse because you like its name, but other approaches work better with mutual funds.

While you probably don't want to risk choosing funds for your 401(k) portfolio by their names alone, the words that describe a fund can give you a sense of the types of investments the fund makes or the manager's investment style.

Along with the funds that fit neatly into the stock pile, the bond pile, and the money market pile, your plan may offer one or more index funds, a balanced fund, or funds identified by words like value, blend, international, or global.

INDEX FUNDS
Mirror market index performance

fees are significantly lower than the fees on managed funds.

Since most indexes include a large number of securities, they automatically provide a degree of diversification. And, in a strong market, the performance of an index fund is similarly strong—though not every fund that tracks the same index delivers the exact same return as the index, or as other funds tracking that index.

On the other hand, in a weak market, an index fund can't deliver a stronger performance than the market it is tracking, while a managed fund can. In fact, managed funds may do significantly better than index funds in volatile markets as well.

The other major limitation of an index fund may be that it isn't as diversified as you might imagine. If the index being tracked is market-capitalization weighted—and most are—the performance of a very few large-cap stocks drives what happens to the index. In 1999, for example, the entire gain in the S&P 500 was produced by the performance of just 31 stocks.

INDEX FUNDS
An **index fund** is designed to mirror the performance of a specific market index, either by owning all of the stocks or bonds in that index or by selecting a representative sampling that will produce parallel results.

The most common index funds in 401(k) plans track the Standard & Poor's 500-stock Index (S&P 500), generally considered the benchmark for large-cap stock performance, or the Lehman Brothers Aggregate Bond Index, the standard for evaluating the performance of investment-grade corporate and government bonds. Some funds also offer a broader-based fund, such as one tracking the Wilshire 5000, which includes all stocks trading on the major US markets.

THUMBS UP OR DOWN
Index funds may be appealing choices for many reasons. Since there are few buy and sell decisions—the fund's portfolio changes only when the securities in the index it's tracking change—you may feel insulated from a manager's potential miscalculations, such as selling a stock too soon or too late. In addition, index fund

A WORD TO THE WISE
It's easier to make investment choices if you know what the key words mean.

A **blended fund** buys several types of funds within a particular asset class. For example, a growth fund might buy both large-cap and small-cap stocks, or a small-cap fund might buy some value stocks and some growth stocks.

BALANCED FUNDS

Balanced funds are the ultimate in diversified investing. Their managers buy stocks, preferred stocks, and bonds in order to provide both long-term growth in value and some current income. Because stocks tend to provide strong returns in different market environments than bonds do, and vice versa, a fund that owns some of each is usually less volatile than a strictly stock or bond fund.

When stock markets are in a slump, a balanced fund tends not to lose as much value as a stock fund because it continues to collect income from its bond investments. And, as an added plus, that income can be reinvested, perhaps at bargain prices.

One of the trade-offs for minimizing volatility is that, in a bull market, a balanced fund doesn't produce as strong a return as a stock fund. And balanced funds can be disappointing when interest rates are rising, since both stock and bond prices tend to suffer.

While there's no rule about the proportions that make a balanced fund balanced, a 60% stock to 40% bond ratio is common. Most funds establish certain limits—requiring that at least 25% of the fund be invested in bonds and 25% in stocks, for example—and let the fund manager shift the holdings to make the most of changing market conditions. You can find those limits, and a description of the fund manager's style, in the fund's prospectus.

BALANCED FUNDS
Include both stock and bond investments

A **core fund** buys securities within a clearly defined market segment, such as large-cap growth or small-cap value.

An **emerging markets fund** buys stock in corporations in developing countries because the manager expects those economies to produce rapid growth.

A **high-yield fund**, sometimes known less politely as a junk bond fund, buys low-rated corporate bonds that pay higher than average interest rates to offset a greater than average risk of default.

An **international fund** buys securities in markets other than the US.

A **global fund** buys securities in countries around the world, including the US. In fact, some global funds invest up to 75% of their assets in US markets.

A **value fund** buys stocks that the manager considers underpriced and expects to rebound in value.

Brokerage Accounts

Some 401(k) plans open a window to broad investment opportunities.

Some 401(k) plans let you invest in stocks, bonds, or mutual funds of your choosing, as well as the funds and company stock that are part of the plan's menu. Using this option, you trade through a designated brokerage account, just as you would using a broker outside the plan.

PROS

- **Greatest possible investment choices**
- **Capital gains aren't subject to current taxes**

THE RISK OF FLYING SOLO

Investing your 401(k) money through a brokerage account, or window, has advocates as well as detractors.

Those in favor argue that having the greatest possible choice is a boon for 401(k) participants with investment experience who prefer to select their own investments and have the skill and experience to do it.

But others believe that having unlimited choice may be confusing or intimidating. They point out that it's impossible for plan sponsors to evaluate the nearly infinite array of investments that are available through brokerage accounts. They also worry that employees may not have enough information to make smart choices.

Some employers fear that they might be held legally liable for losses if plan participants are disappointed with their returns, since any investments made through the plan might appear to have been sanctioned by the employer.

A TAX PLUS

From the employee's perspective, one of the greatest appeals of a 401(k) brokerage account is that capital gains aren't subject to current taxes. For example, if a stock in your portfolio hit a new high in a period of market exuberance, you could sell it and realize the profit without having to turn over 20% to Uncle Sam. You could then use the entire amount to make more stock investments, or earmark some of the gain for a more conservative account as insurance against a downturn (or a bad investment decision).

Of course, there's also the possibility with a 401(k) brokerage account that you could lose large amounts of money if the markets faltered or you made poor choices. In that case, you can't write off any of those capital losses to offset gains.

While you defer tax on any capital gains you realize in a 401(k) brokerage account, remember that you do pay income tax when you start withdrawing from your account. Currently, those rates are higher than the capital gains rate.

But over long periods of time, the additional money your investment earnings could generate has the potential to offset this additional tax.

A TRADING PRICE TAG

Maintaining a brokerage account carries a modest annual fee—in the range of $25 to $175, depending on the firm. Further, you may pay transaction costs and commissions on each trade you make. Most people who are enthusiastic about the chance to invest their 401(k) money as they please consider those charges worth the price.

Similarly, mutual funds you purchase through a brokerage account may have higher fees than those provided by your employer, in part because your employer may subsidize part of the cost of investing or because the choices offered through the plan are institutional funds, which typically have lower fees. Investors are responsible for paying transaction costs, as well as annual fees.

Mutual fund from your employer

Mutual fund brokerage account

CONS

- **May not have all the information needed to make good choices**
- **Short-term trading can jeopardize long-term retirement goals**

THROWING MONEY OUT THE WINDOW

Some financial advisers object to offering brokerage accounts in 401(k) plans because they worry that some investors might be tempted to try short-term trading, also known as **day trading**. Day traders attempt to make money on rapid, short-term price changes in a number of different stocks. But they face the increased risk of substantial losses by trying to time their trades. Further, the critics say, stressing short-term gains is at odds with the goal of retirement savings, which is long-term growth.

Similarly, these same critics fear that being able to trade regularly in a 401(k) brokerage account might encourage less experienced investors to sell off stocks during a market downturn and buy them again when the markets head back up.

Experts believe that this approach—which they sometimes describe as a knee jerk reaction to market fluctuations—is a bad idea. It means you pay higher prices when you repurchase shares, on top of sustaining losses, if you sell when share prices have declined—precisely the point at which panic tends to set in.

There's lots of statistical evidence to show that investors who stay in the market through thick and thin can ride out market swings and come out ahead of investors who move in and out—often missing major gains as a result.

LETTING THE LIGHT IN

The opportunity to choose among a larger universe of mutual funds or to trade stocks and bonds in your 401(k) account is sometimes described as a window.

Variable Annuities

Annuities can open up another 401(k) investment track.

Variable annuities are another way to put your retirement savings to work. They may appear as menu items in your 401(k) along with mutual funds, stable value funds, and other choices. Or, if your plan provider is an insurance company, the plan itself may be a variable annuity.

A SECOND ROUND OF CHOICES

When you put money into a 401(k), you typically divide your contribution among several of the investment alternatives—one of which may be a variable annuity. If you choose the variable annuity, you then make another round of choices to allocate your contribution among different funds (often called separate accounts, subaccounts, or investment portfolios) that the annuity offers. Your choices may include several equity funds, a fixed-income fund, and a money market fund.

As your contribution goes into the annuity, you buy **accumulation units**, based on the accumulation unit value, which is the net asset value (NAV) of the fund adjusted for expenses. Any earnings in your annuity funds, which are based on the performance of the underlying investments, are reinvested to buy more units of the funds and build the value of your annuity.

A DOUBLE LIFE

Like mutual funds, variable annuities have a life outside 401(k) plans. You can buy a variable annuity on your own with aftertax dollars, just as you can buy a mutual fund. But unlike mutual fund earnings, which are taxable in the year you earn them, all variable annuities are considered retirement savings plans, and their earnings always accumulate tax deferred.

The chief differences between qualified annuities, meaning those that are included in a qualified plan like a 401(k), and their nonqualified siblings, are the rules governing contributions and withdrawals.

When an annuity is qualified, you can invest pretax dollars up to the annual cap established by the government or the limit your employer allows, but no more. And you must begin withdrawing from your plan when you stop working or reach 70½—whichever comes later.

When an annuity is unqualified, you can add as much money as you choose each year, but you contribute aftertax income, or money on which you have paid income tax. On the plus side, though, there aren't any federal rules about the age at which you must start withdrawing (though state rules may say 85 or 90). That gives you more control over how to balance withdrawals from your accounts each year.

ANNUITY CHOICES

If you concentrate on the equity funds that a variable annuity offers, you take the same types of risk as when you buy stock mutual funds. And you have the potential for the same level of return before fees.

When the stock market is strong, your funds may increase significantly in value and move you forward toward the goal of accumulating a large retirement account. When the market falters, however, or the type of fund you've chosen doesn't provide strong returns, your account value may shrink.

You may also be able to choose bond or money market funds within your annuity, although many experts suggest that concentrating on growth is a better strategy for a variable annuity than protecting principal.

INSURANCE PROTECTION

One thing that sets variable annuities apart from other 401(k) alternatives is that annuities promise a guaranteed death benefit. If you die during the time you're putting money into your account, the annuity issuer pays your beneficiaries at least the **principal**, or amount you put into the annuity over time. Certain annuities lock in gains as well, increasing the death benefit to reflect the value of the contract at either its highest value or its most recent valuation.

However, this protection can make a variable annuity more expensive than investing directly in the mutual funds or other investments offered in your 401(k). And critics question its actual benefit.

INCOME FOR LIFE

If you put your retirement savings into a variable annuity, when you retire you'll be able to convert your accumulated account value into a stream of retirement income that will continue as long as you live. If you choose a joint and survivor payment plan, the income will last for two lifetimes, yours and your beneficiary's.

The income can be fixed, which means that you'll receive the same amount in each payment. You can also choose variable income, which means that the amount you get changes from payment to payment to reflect the return on the annuity's underlying investments. The appeal of variable income payments is that they have the potential to increase over time.

RANGE OF POSSIBILITIES

MUTUAL FUNDS   COMPANY STOCK   GIC

MY INVESTMENTS

ADDED INSURANCE

Though variable annuities are insurance company products, the money you contribute does not go into the insurance company accounts the way money you spend for a fixed annuity or life insurance policy does. Instead, your assets are held in a separate account and are not at risk if the insurer defaults. That doesn't mean, though, that you're protected against investment losses within the individual funds you select.

Company Stock

Sometimes buying what you know is a smart investment strategy—and sometimes it's not.

If you work for a publicly traded corporation, the list of investment choices in your 401(k) plan may include the opportunity to buy company stock or put money into a company stock fund.

You may even find there are incentives to encourage you to make this choice. For example, you may be able to purchase the stock at a price that's lower than the current market price. Or, you may be able to put in a higher percentage of your pay if you choose company stock. And, in certain instances, the amount you choose to invest in company stock can determine the percentage of the match you receive.

In fact, some employers make their entire matching contribution in the form of stock instead of cash. If that's the case, your account is credited with company stock or shares in a company stock fund, no matter how your individual contributions are invested.

DRAWING FROM THE SAME WELL

It may be a smart choice to invest in your company's stock. After all, you probably understand the products and services, what the company's doing to expand its business opportunities and market share, and the strengths or weaknesses of its management. Those are exactly the kinds of things you investigate when you're considering any stock investment. And investing in your employer's stock gives you an opportunity to share in the success you're contributing to as an employee.

When you invest in your company's stock, you may get...

Better 401(k) matching

Tax advantages

An increase in your 401(k) cap

% you invest in employer's stock

WEIGHING IN

When you receive matching contributions in the form of company stock, an increasingly large percentage of your total portfolio may be in a single investment. In fact, in plans where this matching arrangement is in place, the typical employee has about a third of his or her portfolio allocated to employer's stock.

Some experts argue that acquiring

On the other hand, you already depend on your employer for your current income. If you have a defined benefit retirement plan in addition to your 401(k), the company will also be providing part of your retirement income. So you might want to think twice about tying your financial security too tightly to a single source.

In the worst possible circumstance, if your employer went out of business, you might not only be out of a job, but the portion of your 401(k) that's invested in company stock might be worthless. Even if you can't imagine such a disaster really happening, it can be one of the potential drawbacks of this 401(k) investment choice.

SOME TAX ADVANTAGES

If company stock increases in value during the time it's in your plan (as you hope it will), you may be able to postpone paying tax on the gain by withdrawing the stock from the plan rather than moving it to a rollover IRA with other plan assets.

If you take the stock out, you owe income tax on only its value when it was added to your account, not on any increase in value. You owe no additional tax as long as you hold onto the stock.

And, when you do sell, you may be eligible to pay tax on any increase in value at the lower capital gains rate. In fact, selling company stock is the only current exception to the rule that all withdrawals

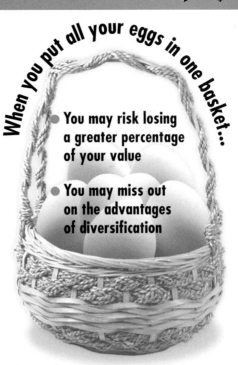

When you put all your eggs in one basket...

- You may risk losing a greater percentage of your value

- You may miss out on the advantages of diversification

from retirement plans are taxed at your regular income tax rate. But the rules are tricky, so be sure you get expert professional advice.

STOCK OWNERSHIP, TWO

Choosing to buy company stock with your 401(k) contributions is different from getting stock from your employer through an **employer stock ownership plan (ESOP)**. An ESOP, which generally has been approved as a retirement plan by the IRS, is a trust to which the company contributes shares of newly issued stock, shares the company has held in reserve, or the cash to buy stock. The shares go into individual accounts set up for employees who meet the plan's eligibility requirements—generally the same ones that determine eligibility for a 401(k).

In fact, while an ESOP may be separate from a 401(k), it may also be part of the same plan. If it's linked, your employer may match your contribution by adding shares to your ESOP account rather than adding cash to your investment account. In many cases, matches made through ESOPs are more generous, in part because there are tax advantages to using an ESOP and in part because an ESOP can be a good way to attract interest in—and contributions to—the plan.

If you leave your job, you have the right to sell your shares, on the open market if your employer is a public company or back to the ESOP at fair market value if it's not. About 90% of companies offering ESOPs are privately held.

Low prices on stock

stock in a well-regarded company strengthens your 401(k) portfolio whether you work for the company or not. Others feel that diversification is always preferable, no matter how attractive the stock may be.

Portfolio Building

There are secrets to making smart 401(k) investments, but no mystery.

A 401(k) portfolio is a collection of investments you assemble by selecting among the choices your plan offers. The best portfolio is one that produces the strongest possible long-term growth at the level of risk you're comfortable taking. You can make portfolio changes as investment alternatives are added, as you get closer to retirement, and also as market conditions change.

FIGURING WHAT YOU'LL NEED

To calculate the income you'll need for retirement, you'll need to account for:

- Your current salary
- The number of years until you plan to retire
- The amount you have already saved
- The potential inflation rate
- The estimated real rate of return, or what you can expect to earn on your investments after adjusting for inflation

You can use a retirement planning calculator to help you figure out what you'll need. These calculators are available online on many financial services sites. Check your mutual fund company, bank, broker, or insurance company, or a site that specializes in 401(k)s.

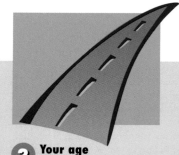

Getting Started

Building a strong 401(k) portfolio isn't easy. But it's worth the time and effort it takes. Whether you're making investment decisions for the first time, or as part of getting your retirement savings portfolio in shape, you'll want to consider five key factors:

1 Other retirement assets
It's important to know what portion of your long-term retirement planning your 401(k) account represents. If it's just one part of a total portfolio that includes an individual retirement account (IRA), taxable investments, and perhaps a pension or deferred annuity, you may be comfortable concentrating your 401(k) contributions in just one or two of the best-performing alternatives your plan offers.

But if it's the only money you're putting away for retirement, you may want to balance your portfolio, seeking the greatest possible growth while diversifying to reduce risk.

2 Your age
If you have many years of work ahead of you, you can afford to take greater risks with your 401(k) account. You may want to invest the bulk of your money in stock mutual funds and perhaps a small percentage in company stock, if it's available. If an investment doesn't perform well for a period—because the manager's investment style is out of favor or a certain category of stocks is in a slump—you'll have time to recoup the loss.

On the other hand, if you're planning to retire fairly soon, you may want to gradually shift at least some of your assets into less volatile investments to **preserve capital**, or hold on to what you've got. Remember, though, that it's important to keep at least a portion of your assets focused on growth even after you retire.

3 Your future income needs
Projecting your future income needs can tell you how aggressively or conservatively you should invest. Experts agree that you're likely to need at least 70% to 80% of your final preretirement income to live comfortably after you stop working.

You'll want to figure out how much of that amount will come from other sources, including any pension, individual retirement plan, or annuity payments you may

BASIC STRATEGIES

To get a feel for putting a 401(k) portfolio together, take a look at these three sample combinations. Each is designed to show a level of risk-taking that might be appropriate at a particular stage in your career. Unless you invest your 401(k) using a brokerage account, and purchase individual securities, these allocations apply to mutual funds available through your plan.

MODEL ALLOCATIONS

	large-company stocks	small-company stocks	international stocks	balanced funds	long-term bonds	money market
20 or more years to retirement	40%	35%	15%	10%	—	—
10 to 20 years to retirement	35%	20%	15%	20%	20%	—
5 years or less to retirement	30%	10%	—	20%	30%	10%

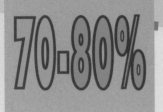

70-80%

be eligible for, plus what Social Security will provide. Everyone over 25 who is part of the Social Security system gets an annual statement with an estimate of that amount. If you're younger than 25, you can request a copy.

4 Your tolerance for risk
The risk-return tradeoff you're willing to make is a key element in your investment decisions, both inside and outside your 401(k). It's a well-known fact that investments posing a greater risk to your principal offer potentially greater returns—along with a greater probability of losses, at least in the short term.

If you're not comfortable assuming any risk, it's best to recognize that fact—and its consequences—early on. But if you put

most of your contributions in more liquid investments, you run up against inflation risk and the very real possibility that your buying power won't keep up with your spending needs.

5 Your current tax bracket
If your current federal income tax bracket is 31% or higher, you may want to use your 401(k) account for dividend- and interest-paying investments and make long-term growth investments in taxable accounts outside the plan. That way, any current earnings compound tax deferred, and you can postpone tax on the growth investments until you sell at some point in the future. You'll owe tax on these earnings at the lower capital gains rate rather than at your federal income tax rate. This lower rate doesn't apply to investment earnings you eventually withdraw from a retirement savings plan.

Understanding Investment Risk

You can take some risks and still sleep at night.

Every investment carries some risk. But what can be confusing, and more than a little frustrating, is that all risks are not alike. Just as soon as you think you've sidestepped one problem, you may come face to face with another.

The risk that may seem the most obvious—and also the most frightening—is the risk of losing money. If you invest $5,000 to buy 100 shares of a stock when it costs $50 a share, and a month later it's selling for $35 a share, your investment portfolio is worth $1,500 less. Or if you use your $5,000 to buy a bond and the issuer defaults, you're likely to lose some, and maybe all, of your money.

But there may be more serious risks than short-term drops in value. Perhaps the most dangerous is one that creeps up on everyone: the impact of inflation. You don't lose money with inflation. But you do lose buying power.

If you have $5,000 in a savings account earning 5% interest, you'll collect $250 a year in income, or a little more if the interest is compounded. But after 10 or 15 years, the $250 you earn each year won't buy what it once did. In fact, it probably won't even come close. That's because money historically loses value over time as the prices of goods and services rise.

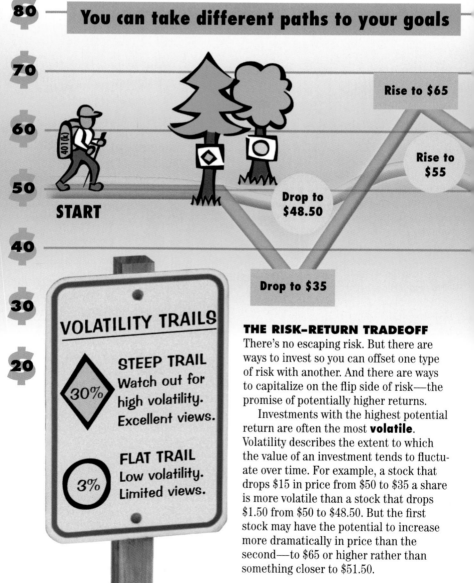

You can take different paths to your goals

Rise to $65

Rise to $55

Drop to $48.50

START

Drop to $35

VOLATILITY TRAILS

STEEP TRAIL
30% Watch out for high volatility. Excellent views.

FLAT TRAIL
3% Low volatility. Limited views.

THE RISK-RETURN TRADEOFF

There's no escaping risk. But there are ways to invest so you can offset one type of risk with another. And there are ways to capitalize on the flip side of risk—the promise of potentially higher returns.

Investments with the highest potential return are often the most **volatile**. Volatility describes the extent to which the value of an investment tends to fluctuate over time. For example, a stock that drops $15 in price from $50 to $35 a share is more volatile than a stock that drops $1.50 from $50 to $48.50. But the first stock may have the potential to increase more dramatically in price than the second—to $65 or higher rather than something closer to $51.50.

THE PRICE OF LIQUIDITY

You may find yourself facing the dilemma of wanting or needing to sell an investment for less than you think it's worth. While equity investments are **liquid**, in the sense that you can almost always sell when you want, their prices aren't guaranteed.

A liquid investment changes very little in value over time. For every dollar you put into a savings account, a certificate of deposit (CD), or other insured account, you can usually take a dollar out. Money market mutual fund managers strive to provide that same liquidity. The tradeoff for this safety is slower growth and the possibility that your real return will be so minimal that you won't accumulate enough assets to live comfortably.

Perhaps the greatest risk to portfolio growth is an illiquid investment that provides a limited return. One 401(k) example is a fixed-income investment that charges a large redemption fee if you want to take your money out. Although this type of investment may protect you from volatility, you're sacrificing both potential return and the flexibility to make changes in your portfolio.

Choosing volatile investments can lead you on a bumpier road than sticking with investments that are more stable in price. But the added risk comes with the potential for greater long-term growth.

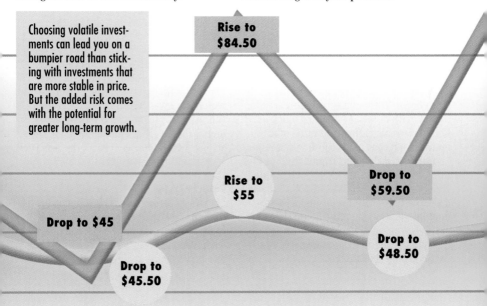

Rise to $84.50

Rise to $55

Drop to $59.50

Drop to $45

Drop to $45.50

Drop to $48.50

What volatility means to you is that if you sell when the price is down—whether because you need the money, you're worried about further drops, or for any other reason—you'll lose money.

TIME CONQUERS (ALMOST) ALL

Using time to your advantage can help you minimize risk and still reap the return that certain volatile investments can provide.

When you consider a stock or stock mutual fund, ask yourself if you plan to keep it in your portfolio for an extended period, barring any unforeseen developments such as a management change or an acquisition. The longer you hold a volatile investment, the better the chance it will be worth more than you paid for it.

Here's one look at how volatility works: Suppose a stock drops 30%—from $50 to

$35 a share—then rebounds to $50, and gains another 30%, to $65. The next time it drops 30%, or $19.50, it's new low is $45.50, not $35. Eventually the rebound from a 30% drop plus a new gain produce a price that can be significantly higher than the starting price.

Of course, stock price movements aren't always as neat as this hypothetical example makes them seem. But the principle is valid: Over time, prices in general go up.

Remember, though, that some volatile investments—such as commodity futures contracts—don't get less risky over time, at least in part because the period you own the investment is fairly short. Others, like high-yield bonds, are likely to be as risky throughout their term as they are when you buy them.

Risk Strategies

Recognizing the threats to your goals can help you figure out diversionary tactics.

You face two categories of risk as you build and maintain your 401(k) portfolio. **Investment risk** refers to the potential loss of value in individual stocks, bonds, mutual funds, or other investments. **Portfolio risk** results from owning a particular combination of investments.

INVESTMENT RISK

No matter how you structure your 401(k) portfolio, there's no getting around some degree of investment risk:

Company risk is the possibility of losing money on a stock because of investors' changing perceptions. For example, since the value of a stock depends on what investors are willing to pay for it, a negative reaction to company events, such as lower than expected earnings, can drive the price down. The same is true, to a smaller extent, with bonds. And falling stock or bond prices also affect the value of a mutual fund that holds these investments.

Market risk stems from a drop in the overall value of the stock or bond markets. Many factors, economic and political, can drive the markets down or make them fluctuate at any time. And when the value of the market as a whole declines, so does the value of the individual investments that make up that market.

Interest-rate risk refers to the fact that existing bonds and bond funds lose value when interest rates rise. Bond prices and interest rates move in opposite directions. So when rates go up, the total return on a bond—its yield plus gain or loss in price—falls.

Credit risk is the possibility that a bond issuer won't be able to make regular interest payments or repay your principal when the investment matures. You face the same risk with fixed annuities or other fixed-income investments. You have a defense against this risk though, since issuers are regularly rated for creditworthiness.

Currency risk affects your overseas investments. As the exchange rate between the US dollar and the currencies in which the investments are sold fluctuates, the value of your return on these investments reflects that change. In brief, the stronger the dollar is abroad, the less your investment will be worth.

PORTFOLIO RISK

Creating a strong portfolio is a more difficult task than choosing one or two individual investments. That's because when you put together a group of investments, you have to consider the way

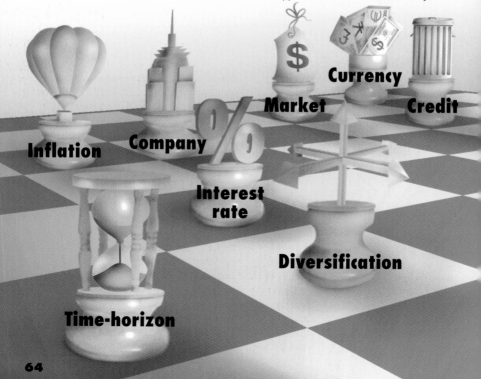

Currency

Market

Credit

Inflation

Company

Interest rate

Diversification

Time-horizon

they'll interact and what the overall effect will be on the growth of your retirement savings.

Inflation risk is perhaps the most serious portfolio risk you can take. If your reaction to investment risk is to choose primarily safe investments that promise a set return, you run the risk that your retirement savings will not provide enough long-term growth to meet your financial needs.

Diversification risk—more accurately nondiversification risk—can also threaten your portfolio. If you concentrate too much money in one or two investments, you're more vulnerable to loss of value than you are if you have several investments that may respond differently to changing economic conditions. Of course, diversification by itself is no guarantee of investment success.

Company stock risk is the danger of owning too much stock in your employer's company. In the first place, it's an example of diversification risk. And it links the growth of your retirement portfolio much too closely to your primary source of current income. If your employer matches your contribution with stock, or requires you to buy stock to qualify for a matching contribution, it's important to emphasize diversification in all of your other investments.

Time-horizon risk means jeopardizing your long-term savings by shifting your investments too often. Not only do you risk being in the wrong investments at the wrong time, but each time you buy or sell

an investment, the transaction costs reduce the value of your portfolio. As more employers offer the option to switch your investments on a daily basis, time-horizon risk is likely to become a bigger threat.

RISK AND RETURN

Different categories of investments, also called asset classes, pose different levels of risk and related levels of return.

Stocks and stock mutual funds have historically provided the strongest returns, according to data compiled by Ibbotson Associates. Large-company stocks, for example, produced an average total return of 11.3% annually between January 1926 and December 1999, compared with 5.6% for long-term corporate bonds and 3.8% for Treasury bills.

However, in periods when large-company stocks faltered, they also exposed investors to big short-term losses. In 1931, they dropped, as a whole, more than 43% in value and in 1974, they finished the year down more than 26%. Small-company losses have been more dramatic and more frequent, though their long-term total return averaged 12.6% in the same 74-year period. In contrast, the biggest one-year drop in value for long-term corporate bonds was 8.09% in 1969, a year when large-cap stocks dropped 8.5% and small caps, 25.05%.

Company stock

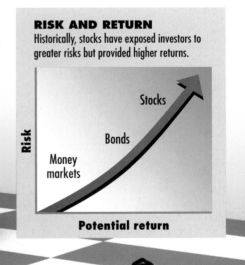

RISK AND RETURN

Historically, stocks have exposed investors to greater risks but provided higher returns.

Risk

Stocks

Bonds

Money markets

Potential return

Asset Allocation

You can slice your 401(k) portfolio to suit your taste.

Asset allocation is an investment strategy for spreading your money across three major asset classes—stocks, bonds, and cash—or the mutual funds that invest in them. Market history shows that if one class of investments is performing poorly, chances are the others are doing better. So by investing in all three, you limit your risk and improve your chances of a higher long-term return.

Asset allocation is a three-step process.

1 You sketch out the mix of asset classes you think is right for your portfolio.

2 You assign a percentage of the portfolio's total value to each class.

3 You buy investments to fill in the percentages you've selected for each asset class.

For example, if you allocate 60% of your contribution to a stock fund, and you put $400 from each paycheck into your 401(k), then $240 of each contribution goes into the stock fund ($400 x 60% = $240).

CLASS ACTIONS

When you're putting money into a 401(k), you're really concerned with just three asset classes:
- Equity investments, including stocks and stock mutual funds
- Fixed-income investments, including bonds and bond mutual funds
- Capital preservation investments, including money market funds and stable value funds

10% Fixed income

80% Equity

10% Capital preservation

KEEPING TRACK

You can track asset allocation in your 401(k). Your account statement reports the percentage of your total contribution that goes into each investment. And you can estimate whether the actual value of your investments is in line with the allocation you've chosen by dividing the current value of each investment class by the total value of your account.

Current value of class
÷ Total value of account
= **% of asset allocaton**

RUNNING THE NUMBERS

Which asset allocation should you choose? First and foremost, you need to consider your investment goals. If your target is maximum long-term growth, as it is for most of the time you're putting money into a 401(k) account, you'll probably want to put the greatest emphasis on growth investments, specifically stocks and stock mutual funds. If you're ready to begin withdrawing from your account, you may want to gradually shift the proportion of stocks and bonds or other fixed-income securities, so that more of your assets are price-stable and produce more regular income.

Next, you might look at the asset allocation models that financial institutions recommend. They can give you a sense of what the experts are thinking. Then work with your financial adviser to design an allocation model that suits your age, retirement plans, and risk tolerance.

You can also create an allocation model using retirement planning software available from mutual fund companies and brokerage firms. Or try the retirement planning tools available on a number of financial websites.

THERE'S NO RIGHT ALLOCATION

No single allocation model produces strong results in all economic climates, so experts suggest different models at different times. Even models suggested at the same time may differ from each other, sometimes subtly and sometimes significantly. Likewise, your strategy may differ dramatically from what other people are doing.

For example, conventional wisdom suggests that the further away you are from retirement, the greater the investment risk you should assume. This approach isn't right for everyone, however.

Say you're in your early 30s. If you were to follow the guidelines for people 20 or more years away from retirement, you would invest 80% or more of your 401(k) account in stocks and stock mutual funds. But if the prospect of a bear market—a sustained downturn in the value of stocks—makes you very uneasy, you may choose to limit your stock allocation to 60% of your account.

On the other hand, suppose you're in your 60s. According to conventional guidelines, you should have around 30% of your account invested in stocks. But if Social Security, your pension benefits, and the part-time work you're planning to do will cover most of your expenses right after retirement, you may want to be more aggressive with your 401(k) money. So, you might invest a larger portion— perhaps 60%—in stocks, with the thought that you can always reallocate later. In fact, unless your 401(k) is still in a former employer's plan, and you can't make changes to the account, you'll be able to adjust your allocation when you feel it's important. Remember, you're making a long-term commitment to saving for retirement, not to specific investments or asset classes.

30% Capital preservation

30% Equity

30% Fixed income

NUMBER GAMES

You can see the impact of asset allocation by examining the results of three hypothetical $100,000 portfolios invested in different ways. The return on the stock-heavy portfolio (A) for just one year, even before compounding begins to intensify the gap, is roughly 43% greater than the portfolio emphasizing cash (C).

The one-year return for each portfolio is calculated using the average total return for three major asset classes—11.3% for large-cap stocks, 5.6% for long-term corporate bonds, and 3.8% for cash—between January 1926 and December 1999.

One-year return

$10,000 — **$9,980**
$9,000 —
$8,000 —
$7,000 — **$7,520**
$6,000 —
$5,000 — **$5,660**

	Portfolio A	Portfolio B	Portfolio C
STOCKS	80%	40%	20%
BONDS	10%	40%	20%
CASH	10%	20%	60%

Diversification

You can knit together a diversified portfolio of investments.

Putting part of your 401(k) contribution into equities, part into fixed-income investments, and perhaps part into cash is only the first step in creating your 401(k) portfolio. Unless you have a limited choice, you'll need to decide among investments within those classes in order to create a **diversified** portfolio. That means identifying subclasses of investments within each of the three asset classes.

For example, even though a fund that buys small-company stock and a fund that buys stock in large companies are both equity funds, they are significantly different investments. Each one exposes you to different levels of risk, changes in value at different rates, and may prosper in different economic circumstances. So when small-company stocks are providing stronger returns than large-company stocks, a small-company fund is likely to provide a stronger return than a large-company fund, and vice versa.

If you own each type of fund, you're positioned to benefit from a strong return on at least a portion of your portfolio, no matter which fund is providing the stronger performance at any given time. That's the whole point of diversification: It means you're investing to protect your portfolio against major losses that could result from a drop in value of a single investment or market sector.

In other words, a diversified portfolio contains investments that are not only individually strong, but also distinctly different from each other. That way, your portfolio has a better chance of providing strong performance in a variety of situations.

IF YOUR TIMING IS OFF

While the ups and downs of investment performance are clearly recognizable, it's almost impossible to predict when they might occur. If you try to **time the market**—for example, if you wait to buy until exactly the moment you think an investment is about to take off, you run the risk of being out of the market when the price increases most. And you'll end up paying more to own it.

THE SEESAW PRINCIPLE

Diversification works because the major asset classes tend to move in opposite directions. So do the subclasses within them.

For example, when investors are buying stocks, stocks provide a strong return and bond returns are likely to be weaker. And when investors get out of the stock market and buy bonds, bond returns generally strengthen and stock returns weaken. Similarly, there are times when overseas stocks (and the mutual funds that invest in them) provide stronger returns than stocks in US companies. At other times, domestic stocks are on top.

If you keep money invested in a variety of asset classes and subclasses, you can benefit in two ways. First, you're in a position to profit from strong returns in a particular subclass. Second, those gains can help offset losses in a class or subclass that's slowing down.

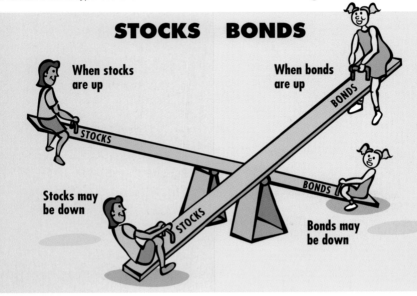

STOCKS BONDS

When stocks are up

When bonds are up

Stocks may be down

Bonds may be down

USING VARIETY WISELY

If your 401(k) plan offers just one fund in each asset class, making decisions is simpler than it might otherwise be. Carry out your allocation strategy with the options you have, even if you can't diversify within it. Just make sure you diversify elsewhere in your overall portfolio.

If you have several fund choices within a single asset class—say several stock funds—look first at each fund's investment objective. Try to avoid investment in several funds all making the same type of investment.

While a fund's name is often a useful clue, don't take it at face value. Look first at the fund's prospectus for its official statement, and then check to see how the fund is classified by research companies, including Lipper Inc. and Morningstar. You may find that a fund that describes itself as a small-company fund actually has substantial investments in medium- and large-sized companies. That could mean you're not as diversified as you'd like to be, and may need to look at other alternatives.

LOOKING FURTHER AFIELD

International investments, especially equities, are also an important part of diversification. Because the world's economies respond primarily to events and conditions in their homelands or regions, investing abroad is a way to build a broad-based portfolio. And the opportunity to invest in emerging as well as developed markets offers a further level of diversification.

While international investing provides diversification simply by raising the number of potential investment choices, it also adds diversity by spreading your investments across different regions of the world. For example, putting money into a European fund or an Asian fund can position you to benefit from potential strength in those areas during periods when the US economy is sluggish or in recession.

In general, mutual funds provide the simplest way to invest internationally, since they handle all of the currency and taxation issues that go along with buying and selling abroad. So if your 401(k) plan offers an international stock fund, you'll probably want to consider it as a potential diversification tool.

Yield and Return

There are different formulas for analyzing success.

There's something satisfying about having your money earn more money. Part of that sense of accomplishment probably comes from knowing that you don't always have to keep your shoulder to the grindstone to get ahead. But you can't just sit back and let things happen. You have to stay alert to the kind of progress you're actually making toward your financial goals.

You can measure what you earn on your investments in two ways, by figuring **yield** and **return**.

YIELD

Yield is what you collect in income on an investment, expressed as a percentage of the amount you spent for your investment. For example, the $60 annual interest payment you get on a bond you bought for $1,000 is a 6% yield.

$	60	Dividends or interest
÷ $	1,000	Amount you invested
=	6%	**Yield**

RETURN

Return, or more precisely total return, is the amount your investment increases in value, plus any income you receive. For example, if you earn $60 on a bond and can sell it for $1,100 instead of the $1,000 you paid for it, your total return is $160 ($60 interest + $100 increase in value = $160).

$	1,100	
− $	1,000	
= $	100	Increase in value
+ $	60	Income from investement
= $	160	**Total return**

PERCENT RETURNS

When you look at an investment's return, you want to know how that return compares to the return on your other investments, so you can figure out whether each is pulling its own weight.

Simply looking at the dollar value of your investment doesn't necessarily tell you how well it's been doing. For one thing, you may have contributed different amounts to your investments when you chose them initially, and you may have added different amounts over time. For example, if all you know is that an investment has increased $1,000 in value, it's hard to evaluate the information—a $1,000 increase on a $1,000 investment is a very different level of return than a $1,000 increase on a $10,000 investment.

That's why you have to compare investments based on their percent return. To do this, you divide the total return (income plus increase in value) by the amount you've invested. So a $1,000 total return on a $1,000 investment is a 100% return, while a $1,000 total return on $10,000 is a 10% return.

You also need to consider how long you've held an investment when you evaluate its performance. For example, an 18% return in one year is very different from an 18% return over three years. You can compare performance

Annual Percent Return

$	160	Total return
÷ $	1,000	Amount you invested
=	16%	**Percent return**
$	16%	Return
÷ $	3	Number of years
=	5⅓%	**Annual percent return**

over time by dividing each investment's percent return by the number of years you've held it. The result is its annual percent return. For example, a 16% return over one year is a 16% annual percent return, while a 16% percent return over three years is a 5⅓% annual percent return.

CURRENT YIELD

Current yield on a fixed-income investment, such as a bond, is the amount you're earning in relation to the current price rather than the amount you invested. It's a useful number for valuing your investments in the current market.

WHEN RETURN IS REAL

In figuring return on your investment, there's another factor you have to take into account—inflation, or the decreasing value of money over time.

Because inflation is persistent, it gradually erodes your buying power. That means you need more income each year simply to maintain the same standard of living you've been enjoying. And the longer into the future you are trying to anticipate the income you'll need, the more you have to be concerned about inflation.

Real return is the return an investment is currently producing minus the current inflation rate. For example, if one of the stock funds in your portfolio reports a one-year return of 18% and inflation is at 3% that year, the real return on your investment is 15% (18% return − 3% inflation = 15% real return). Another way to look at real return is that it's the portion of your return that matters because it measures the rate at which you're staying ahead of inflation.

REAL RETURN

	18%	Total return
−	3%	Inflation rate
=	15%	**Real return**

The importance of real return emphasizes why you shouldn't concentrate too heavily on fixed-income investments in your retirement portfolio. Since the average return on fixed-income investments is already less than the return on equities, inflation has a proportionally greater impact on the real return they provide.

YOU CAN COUNT YOUR CHICKENS

While the actual return you get on an investment isn't final until you sell the investment and figure out where you stand, you can keep a running tally of reinvested earnings and any increases in value by checking your current account value. Remember, though, not to confuse the contributions you're adding to your account with return that the investment itself is generating. If your increased value is equal to the contributions you've added, your investment isn't providing a positive return.

DID YOU REALIZE THIS?

Gains in the value of an investment that exist on paper—as opposed to gains in your pocket or your bank account—are **unrealized gains**. When you sell, your gains, if any, become realized. Realizing a gain means an investment can no longer increase in value, but it also ends the risk that the investment may lose value. You can also have unrealized losses, especially in the short term. And if you sell when an investment is worth less than you paid for it, you realize a loss.

10% OR BUST

While there's no ideal investment return, obviously the higher your return over an extended period of time, the more your retirement savings account can grow.

Some experts suggest aiming for a 10% overall annual return. You can consider the years you do better as icing on the cake. On the other hand, too many years when your return is lower may be cause for concern: If your average return is 6% instead of 10%, your retirement fund probably won't provide the income you need.

Mutual Fund Quotations

If you want information on retail mutual funds, you can find it easily.

Retail mutual funds are an open book, at least when you want to get up-to-date information about their investment objectives, price, and performance. The funds themselves supply their current net asset value (NAV) and the change in value from the previous day to the National Association of Securities Dealers (NASD) at the end of each trading day. That information is reported daily in the financial press for funds with more than 1,000 shareholders or net assets of more than $25 million.

Companies that specialize in mutual fund research, including Lipper Inc.,

Morningstar, Inc., and ValueLine, Inc., use the information from the funds to calculate investment return and to rank funds based on their performance over different time periods. That analysis, along with details of sales charges, fund expenses, and fund size, is summarized monthly, quarterly, and annually in tables like this one, which uses information from Lipper Inc.

Annual expenses report the percentage of your account assets that you pay to the fund each year as management and other fees.

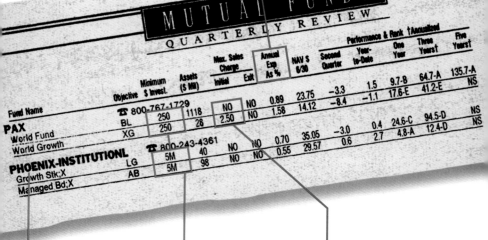

		Minimum $ Invest.	Assets ($ Mil)	Max. Sales Charge		Annual Exp As %	NAV $ 6/30	Second Quarter	Year-to-Date	One Year	Three Yearst	Five Yearst
				Initial	Exit							
Fund Name	Objective	☎ 800-767-1729								1.5	9.7-B 64.7-A	135.7-A
PAX	BL	250	1118	NO	NO	0.89	23.75	−3.3			17.6-E 41.2-E	NS
World Fund	XG	250	28	2.50	NO	1.58	14.12	−8.4	−1.1			
World Growth		☎ 800-243-4361						−3.0	0.4	24.6-C 94.5-D	NS
PHOENIX-INSTITUTIONL	LG	5M	40	NO	NO	0.70	35.05	0.6	2.7	4.8-A 12.4-D	NS
Growth Stk;X	AB	5M	98	NO	NO	0.55	29.57				
Managed Bd;X												

The **mutual fund company name** is followed by the funds it offers, listed in alphabetical order.

When the company name is followed by **institutional**, as Phoenix is, the funds are sold through investment advisers rather than directly to individuals.

If the fund company name appears more than once, followed by an A, B, or other letter, the fund offers different classes of shares. For example, **class A shares** have an initial sales charge and **class B shares** have an exit sales charge.

Minimum $ investment is the amount you need to open an account. That amount can range from as little as the $250 that Pax Funds requires to $5,000 or more. Minimum investments for institutional funds are much higher. The Phoenix funds require $5 million.

Maximum sales charges are charged either when you buy—**initial**—or sell—**exit**—and can be as high at 8.5%, the NASD ceiling, but they rarely are. When **NO** appears, it's a no-load fund that has no sales charges. Some fund companies offer both load and no-load funds, while other companies offer just one or the other. For example, the Pax World fund has no sales charge, while the World Growth fund has an initial charge of 2.5% of the amount you invest.

APPLES TO APPLES

Mutual funds are divided initially into four major categories—stock funds, taxable bond funds, municipal bond funds, and funds that invest in both stocks and bonds. Those categories are then subdivided to account for dozens of distinct objectives.

The most meaningful evaluations you can make of performance, fees, or the other information that's available are by comparing funds that have the same objective: small-cap growth with small-cap growth or long-term bond with long-term bond.

Objective is the fund's investment objective. The firms that analyze mutual fund data group the funds into categories based on the fund's stated objectives or on the type of investments the fund actually makes. For example, the LC describing Price's Blue Chip fund stands for Large-cap Core.

These categories, each with a two-letter abbreviation, are based on classifications developed by Lipper Inc.

Fund Name	Objective	Minimum $ Invest.	Assets ($ Mil)	Max. Sales Charge Initial	Exit	Annual Exp As %	NAV $ 6/30	Second Quarter	Year-to-Date	One Year	Three Years†	Five Years†
☎ 800-231-8432												
RICE FUNDS												
Balanced	BL	2.5K	2052	NO	NO	0.79	19.70	−1.0	1.5	6.0-C	39.1-C	93.9-B
Blue Chip	LC	2.5K	7076	NO	NO	0.91	38.04	0.5	6.9	16.8-B	82.5-B	209.5-A
CA Tx-Fr Bd	SS	2.5K	213	NO	NO	0.58	10.33	1.7	5.0	2.7-B	14.6-A	33.2-A
Cap Apprec	MV	2.5K	787	NO	NO	0.88	13.06	3.6	4.4	2.8-C	26.3-C	74.1-D
Cap Opportunity	XC	2.5K	101	NO	NO	1.26	16.01	−2.6	2.0	13.8-B	45.6-D	104.2-E
Corp Inc	AB	2.5K	44	NO	NO	0.80	8.96	0.8	2.2	2.4-D	13.0-C	NS

NAV is the fund's **net asset value**, or the dollar value of one share of the fund. It's the price the fund pays when you sell your shares. It's figured by adding the value of all of the fund's holdings and dividing by the number of shares. For example, Price Fund's Balanced fund has a NAV of $19.70.

Performance and rank report the percent return in several time periods, from the most recent quarter to as long as five years.

The return for the three- and five-year periods is **annualized**, which means it's computed by dividing the total return for the entire period by the number of years in the period.

When an **NS** appears in a return column, it means that the fund didn't operate for that entire period. Many funds have been opened in the last five years.

The fund is ranked in relation to other funds with the same objective. An "A" indicates a fund whose return was in the top 20%, a "B" indicates the second 20%, and so on.

The rankings, which apply to periods of one year and longer, are sometimes similar over the life of the fund, and sometimes strikingly different. For example, Price's Blue Chip fund ranks A or B in each period, while the company's Capital Opportunity fund drops from a B for the most recent year to an E for five years.

Other companies use different rating or ranking systems than Lipper. Some report a dual ranking, one that ranks a fund against funds with the same objective, and the other that ranks the fund against all funds of the same type, such as all stock funds.

Account Report Cards

Your plan statement provides an in-depth look at where your 401(k) stands.

Your employer is legally required to report the status of your 401(k) account just once a year—and that's only if you request a copy of your statement. Fortunately, however, most plan sponsors automatically provide reports on at least a quarterly basis. Others issue statements monthly. And to keep up with the demand for immediate, up-to-date information, more and more firms are reporting account information online or using automated voice-response units (VRUs).

Regardless of how you get your 401(k) report, it's an important tool for monitoring performance and confirming that deposits are being made.

DOING THE MATH

The timing of the reports you receive depends on how often your plan is valued. Valuation occurs when the plan's recordkeeper reconciles all the activity in your account—such as contributions or matching funds being deposited, the gain or loss from moving assets from one investment option to another, increases or decreases in the value of your investments, and loan repayments you've made—within a particular period.

Armed with increasingly sophisticated electronic tools, recordkeepers have no trouble valuing your account daily and making this important information available to you.

As plans are valued more frequently, you have more flexibility in changing your investment selections—whether your assets are held in plan investments or in brokerage accounts. In most cases, if your plan is valued daily, you can usually switch your current investments and redirect your future plan contributions every day. Similarly, if your plan is valued quarterly, you can usually make changes in your portfolio quarterly as well.

A FRIENDLY VOICE

If you have a touch-tone phone, you can often get 401(k) information using a voice response unit, which is usually accessible through a toll-free telephone number. These systems allow you to access your account balances, investment selections, and personal data, as well as request statements, 24 hours a day, 7 days a week. You usually have to enter an ID number,

Your statement won't look exactly like this one, but it will have this information.

Savings Plan—401(K) Statement

Period: 6/1–9/30

Account To Date	Company Stock (25%)	Equi (50
Employee contributions	$21,312.50	$42,625
Pre-tax	$0.00	$4
After-tax	$2,664.00	$5,32
Company match	$0	$
Rollovers	$23,976.50	$47,95
Totals		

Activity This Period	Company Stock (25%)	Equi (50
Employee contributions	$1,375.00	$2,7
Pre-tax	$3,500.00	
After-tax	$343.75	$
Company match	$0.00	
Withdrawals	$0.00	
Loans	1,000.00	
Transfers in	0.00	-1
Transfers out	$6,218.75	$1
Totals		
Current Totals	**$30,195.25**	**$50,**

Loan information. If you're repaying a loan from your 401(k), the investment from which you took the loan and the

amount that you borrowed will be shown as a debit.

often all or part of your Social Security number, and a personal identification number (PIN).

Voice response units offer the same information that's available in printed form on a statement. The difference is that the systems make it easy for you to reallocate your account—that is, switch your current investments, or change the way your future contributions will be invested—and update personal data.

Remember, though, that the timeliness of your account balance depends on how frequently it's valued. If the recordkeeper performs daily valuations, your account balance will reflect the previous day's clos-

Personal data. You'll find your name, address, date of birth, the date you joined the plan, beneficiaries, and annual salary. If this information is incorrect, check further, as there may also be errors in how your account is valued.

Investment Selections. This section shows your current allocation among the investment options you've chosen. Most plans let you shift your investment mix, though the frequency and timing for making those changes vary from plan to plan, often based on the valuation dates.

Future account value. Some plans may provide a projection of your account's value at retirement based on different hypothetical rates of return, assuming you continue contributing at your current rate.

Vesting status. There may be a statement describing whether or not you are vested in, or own, your employer's contributions to your account, and if not, the date you will become vested.

	anced (0%)	Fixed (25%)	Totals
			$85,250.00
	$0.00	$21,312.50	$0.00
	$0.00	$0.00	$10,656.00
	$0.00	$2,664.00	$0.00
	$0.00	$0.00	$95,906.00
	$0.00	$23,976.50	
			$5,500.00
	$0.00	$1,375.00	$3,500.00
	$0.00	$0.00	$1,375.00
	$0.00	$343.75	$0.00
	$0.00	$0.00	$0.00
	$0.00	$0.00	1,000.00
	0.00	0.00	– 1,000.00
	0.00	0.00	$11,375.00
	$0.00	$1,718.75	
	$0.00	$25,695.25	$106,281.00

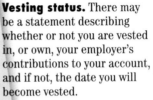

Account balance. The report provides your balance at the beginning and end of the period, plus a breakdown showing your pretax and aftertax contributions (if any), employer contributions (if any), and rollovers from a prior employer's 401(k) plan (if any). If you subtract the total you've added to an investment for the period from its overall increase or decrease in value, you can figure out its rate of return.

Transfers. If you've moved money out of or into your account, those amounts will be reported. For example, you might have added money from a former employer's plan.

PLACE YOUR ORDER
In plans that offer electronic access to account information, you may not receive printed account statements, but you can request them if you wish.

ing prices. But if your plan uses monthly or quarterly valuations, your investments will be priced as of the close of that period.

MAKING CHANGES
The rules for changing your investments differ from plan to plan. Your plan description will tell you how often you can make changes, and when they will take effect. For example, if your plan allows you to switch investments daily, you may have to call or log in by a certain time in order for the change to be implemented the same day. When you make a change, your plan administrator will mail you a confimation statement.

PLANS ONLINE
Online access to 401(k) account information is becoming an increasingly popular feature of many plans. If your plan isn't online yet, it probably will be soon.

Plan websites provide the same account information as printed statements and voice response units in a format that you can view and print at any time. Plan administrators use special software to ensure secure transmission of confidential account information, and require you to identify yourself with a user ID and a password to get access to your account.

Performance Factors

Keeping close tabs on your 401(k) portfolio is critical.

Your 401(k) plan provider's report—whether in print, online, or through a voice response system—will tell you whether your account value went up or down during the period. But you'll need more information to determine whether to stick with your current investment choices as they are or make some changes to improve the chances of meeting your long-term goals.

BENCHMARKS

One of the things you want to know as you evaluate portfolio performance is how well a fund is doing in relation to the other funds making similar types of investments, or striving to achieve a similar goal. That's where benchmarks come in.

A **benchmark** is an index or average that reflects the movement of a particular financial market or market sector. It serves as a standard against which to compare the performance of an investment that belongs to the same market or sector. For example, the Standard & Poor's 500-stock Index (S&P 500) is the benchmark against which the performance of large-capitalization US stocks and stock funds that invest in those stocks are measured. Likewise, the Russell 2000 Index is the standard for small company stocks and funds.

The Lipper Indexes are the standard benchmarks for mutual fund performance. Each of the 29 indexes tracks the performance of funds that invest in a specific group, or subclass, of stocks or bonds, such as large-company growth stocks or US government bonds.

If one of your funds lags behind its appropriate benchmark for more than two or three years, it may be a candidate for replacement. But remember that you can't make a meaningful assessment unless the benchmark you're using is the right one.

ANALYZING STYLE

A fund's **investment style**, which depends on the types of investments it makes, is the most important factor influencing its performance. For example, if a fund invests mainly in bonds, it tends to perform the way the bond market performs. Similarly, a fund that invests in large capitalization stocks tends to perform the way the large-cap segment of the stock market performs.

But not all funds invest in only one segment of the market. For example, a US stock fund might own both large-cap stocks and mid-cap stocks, and keep a percentage of its holdings in cash.

Further, no two funds own exactly the same investments in exactly the same proportions, or produce exactly the same return.

For example, a stock mutual fund that describes itself as a growth fund doesn't necessarily produce the same return as other growth funds. For similar reasons, a growth fund may not produce the same return as an index that tracks growth investments.

To create benchmarks for measuring funds that make diverse investments, companies that specialize in analyzing fund performance use a process called **style analysis** or **returns-based style analysis**. This methodology focuses on the way a fund's returns behave in relation to the returns of a number of different asset classes. That information, in turn, helps to explain the fund's past performance as well as anticipate how the fund is likely to perform in the future.

and passively managed index funds tend to have the lowest fees of all.

Similarly, your account activity, particularly the timing of money flowing into—and sometimes out of—your account, and the costs of the transactions you make, also affect return. For example, if your contribution hits the fund on a day when prices have jumped or dropped, your money will buy a different number of shares than it would have if your purchase had gone through a day earlier or later. And if you do a lot of buying and selling, you may pay substantial sales charges or other fees.

FEES: BE PREPARED
The returns published in the financial press for a particular mutual fund may differ from the return that's reported for the same fund in your portfolio statement. That happens for a number of reasons.

Part of the answer is fees. Unless your employer covers the entire administrative cost of the plan, you may be paying a share of those fees, fees for recordkeeping services your plan offers, or loan fees if you've borrowed from your plan. Those fees are subtracted before your return is reported on your statement.

Fees vary from plan to plan, based in part on who the provider is and in part on the size of the plan. Large plans tend to have lower fees—sometimes much lower—than smaller plans. That's because the more money that flows into the plan, the better the deal the provider is willing to offer to keep the sponsor's business.

OTHER COST ISSUES
Investment management fees, which are figured as a percentage of your assets, are also subtracted before return is reported. Fees for different investments vary, typically based on how active the management is and the kinds of investments the fund makes. For example, stock funds tend to have higher fees than bond funds,

FEE FINDERS
You can get more information about 401(k) fees and expenses from the US Department of Labor. A booklet called "A Look at 401(k) Fees…for Employees" is available on the department's website at www.dol.gov/dol/pwba or by phone at 800-998-7542.

You can also encourage your employer to compare the costs of different 401(k) plans using a form developed by the US Department of Labor and the mutual fund, banking, and insurance industries, all of which sponsor various plans. The form and the Pension and Welfare Benefits Administration's "Study of 401(k) Plan Fees and Expenses" are available from the department.

CHECKING UP ON YOUR OWN
If you're investing in individual stocks or bonds through a 401(k) brokerage account, you'll find that performance data isn't neatly presented to you the way that mutual fund statistics are. But you can find up-to-the-minute information on prices and yields online as well as in the financial pages of major newspapers.

Rebalancing Acts

Keeping your 401(k) portfolio balanced may mean
moving investments around from time to time.

While choosing an asset allocation model
is essential for making the initial investments in your 401(k), that allocation may
not be the best one as time goes by.

Two situations may demand that you
rethink your initial allocation or make
some changes to get back on track:

1 As you get closer to retirement, you
may want to readjust your allocation
strategy to add more stability and emphasize income-producing investments.

2 If market performance increases
or decreases the value of one asset
class so that your actual portfolio allocation is significantly different from the
allocation you selected, you may want
to realign your holdings to get them back
in balance.

KEEPING YOUR BALANCE

Different assets grow at different rates.
Over time, the ones that grow more
quickly will make up a greater percentage
of your portfolio than you originally
planned. For example, to maintain your
portfolio's original asset allocation mix,
you may decide to transfer money from
asset classes that have grown faster—
such as aggressive-growth stock mutual
funds or individual stocks—into those
that have grown more slowly, such as blue
chip funds or capital preservation funds.
If you don't reallocate, you may find yourself with a portfolio that has more risk
or a smaller long-term return than you
originally intended.

One reason many experts suggest you
avoid loading up on your employer's stock
in your 401(k) is that the more shares you
have, the more the stock will influence
your portfolio's equity allocation. As a result, it may be harder to maintain the
balance you want.

GETTING IT DONE

You can rebalance your portfolio in
different ways. They all work, but you may
be more comfortable with one approach
than another.

For example, you can sell off a portion
of the asset class that has increased most
in value and reinvest those profits in the
lagging asset class.

Or you can change the way your future
contributions are allocated, putting more
money into the lagging asset class until
things are back in balance.

You can also add new investments in
the lagging asset class to your portfolio
and funnel your contributions to those
investments.

**It's better not to let your
portfolio get too far out
of balance.**

Blue Chips

A REBALANCING TIMETABLE

Some investment advisers suggest rebalancing your allocation once a year as part of an annual reassessment of your financial plan. But there's no official timetable for rebalancing, and the further in the future your retirement is, the less important frequent rebalancing is likely to be.

Rather than rebalancing mechanically, other experts suggest you might decide to sell off holdings in your portfolio's strongest asset class only when that class exceeds a specific percentage—say 10% or 15%—over your target allocation. That way, you avoid what seems like the backward logic of selling an investment that is doing well in order to put your money into something that seems less likely to help you meet your long-term needs.

Some plan providers may offer a reallocation service, especially if you invest in a **life cycle fund**. Those plans may rebalance as frequently as every quarter, which may be too often. You'll also want to watch the transaction fees in any automatic plan. Programmed rebalancing may eliminate exit fees, but it rarely reduces sales charges.

THE HIDDEN COST OF SHIFTING

If you have online access to your portfolio or you have a 401(k) plan brokerage account, you may be able to shift your asset class allocation and the individual investments within each class as often as you wish.

When your portfolio value is up, you can lock in profits without having to plan for the immediate tax consequences. When it's down, you can move into something safer.

But remember that this kind of constant shifting makes retirement experts shiver. Most trading comes with a price tag, in terms of sales charges and sometimes back-end loads, exchange fees, or exit fees. The more often you trade, the more you pay. So there's a real risk that you may be spending more to make changes than you earn from making them. Even more serious, these experts point out, is that switching out of equities when the equity market drops means you're locking in a loss.

On the other hand, some of the investments in your account may be living up to your expectations, while others are not. Is that the time to make a change? Some experts say that if a mutual or annuity fund produces returns below the average for its category for two years, it's time to sell your shares and put the money into another investment.

WAIT IT OUT

If watching the stock ticker take a nosedive makes you worry that your 401(k) funds are losing value too, or if your account has dropped enough in value to make you uncomfortable, what should you do? In most cases, the answer is to sit tight.

While selling in panic is unprofitable for anyone, experts say it's a particularly bad idea when you're saving for retirement. If you plan to wait 20 years or more before you retire, you'll have time to recoup any current losses. And if you're closer to retirement, you're likely to sacrifice your long-term gains and not have time to rebuild your account.

Mid-cap Stocks

Emerging Stocks

Looking for Guidance

Where's an investor to look for help if past performance can't predict the future?

As you build your 401(k) portfolio, there's no way to be certain what your investments will be worth in the future or how close they'll come to providing the retirement income you'll need. You'll find lots of disclaimers telling you that past performance can't predict future results. So how can you anticipate future returns as accurately as possible?

- Be patient
- Seek knowledge
- Ask questions
- Evaluate advice

ONLINE RESOURCES

Investment companies that sponsor 401(k) plans, and web-based financial sites that specialize in 401(k) advice, may provide online financial planning resources that can help you evaluate how your current portfolio will perform over time and what changes you should consider to maximize your return.

These sites ask you to complete an electronic worksheet or questionnaire that gathers information about you (and your partner if you have one), the investments you currently own, and your contribution rate. You're also asked about your financial goals— at what age you want to

retire, approximately how much money you want to have when you retire, and the level of risk you are comfortable taking.

This information is run through a **Monte Carlo simulation**. This complex mathematical analysis projects thousands of potential outcomes for your investment portfolio, taking a wide range of factors into account, including potential interest rates and inflation rates. By creating so many potential scenarios, these simulations, also

GETTING THE WORD OUT

Many employers worry that providing their 401(k) participants with detailed investment information could be interpreted as providing advice on which investments to make. Specifically, they fear that if employees are unhappy with their portfolio's performances, they might sue on the grounds that they had been misled. So to protect themselves, employers tend to provide minimal information and guidance. Yet, as the number of choices being offered in most plans increases, this lack of information can be a serious handicap.

401(k) Plan Performance
NO ACCESS BEYOND THIS POINT

CAVEAT INVESTOR

Though you can't predict an investment's future performance based on what it did in the past, you can learn valuable lessons from history. That's because stocks, bonds, and other investments don't exist in a vacuum. Their changing values are influenced by any number of unpredictable factors both inside and outside the markets, from investor attitudes to natural disasters.

Just as knowing which party won previous presidential elections can help you speculate about—but not predict—who might win the next time around, knowing the history of an investment can help you anticipate the return it might produce in the future. But history won't let you predict that return with any certainty.

To get more information, you might ask your plan administrator to schedule a meeting or seminar to provide the most recent performance figures on the plan's investment choices. Plan providers, such as mutual fund or insurance companies, may provide discussion leaders for these meetings, or they may have developed a web-based learning center.

IS ONLINE ADVICE FOR YOU?

Online resources can be a useful tool for estimating how your 401(k) portfolio is likely to perform and figuring how to make the best investment choices. They offer a quick, easy way to evaluate where you stand, and because they're online, you can access them whenever you want. Some sites even provide recommendations free of charge.

On the other hand, these sites don't necessarily offer everything you might want from a financial planning resource. For example, some offer only their simpler tools for free, and charge for personalized advice. And some sell investments as well, so it's sometimes important to weigh their recommendations against the potential profit they stand to make from your investment decisions. You might want to find out what a truly impartial online adviser suggests.

One site to investigate for retirement planning worksheets and other planning tools is sponsored by American Savings Education Council (www.asec.org/tools). Another, at www.ebri.org, is sponsored by the Employee Benefit Research Institute.

known as **stochastic modeling** systems, can account for some of the unpredictable but recurrent influences that affect investment performance.

Based on the simulation, the program identifies the most probable outcomes and may recommend that you change your strategy to meet your goals. Alternatively, it may suggest altering your goals to make them more realistic. For example, if your goals is to retire at 50 with $10 million, you might have to think again.

Some sites provide only general advice on how to invest, while others may suggest specific funds to choose. Still others tell you what investments to make for the ideal asset allocation.

OF GAMES AND HEMLINES

Since an investment's past performance can't determine how it will do in the future, some investors have turned to other forms of analysis to help them anticipate the movements of the markets. One tradition, known as the Super Bowl indicator, holds that the stock market will rise or fall based on which football league the winning Super Bowl team is originally from. Another school, called hemline theory, is based on the idea that stock prices rise and fall with the hemlines of women's skirts. While this use of data may be questionable, both methods have devoted followers.

Inside and Outside Your 401(k)

Orchestrating your retirement and regular investing can create financial harmony.

You might think of your retirement savings as a self-contained investment portfolio. You've allocated the assets within your account and made sure your portfolio is diversified. But to make the most of your plan, you also need to think of it as part of your total financial picture.

Even if your contribution to a 401(k) plan is the only active retirement investing you're doing, it probably won't be your only source of retirement income. For example, though Social Security may change over time, it's reasonable to expect some income from that source. You may also be entitled to a pension, even if it's only a modest one. And if you're married, you may get pension income from your spouse's employer. Or, you may own property you can sell or rent.

As you meet your other financial goals, such as buying a home or paying for higher education, or if you have money left over after contributing the maximum to your 401(k), you may be in a position to invest for retirement outside your 401(k) plan.

DON'T FORGET IRA

If your 401(k) is a good one, it's usually smart to put as much money into it as you can. Sometimes, that means coming up against the federal limit—$10,500 in 2001. But when you hit the limit and can afford to salt away more, you might want to consider an individual retirement account (IRA).

While the maximum contribution—$2,000 a year—is considerably lower than the 401(k) limits, IRAs share the 401(k) advantage of tax-deferred growth. That means you postpone tax on any earnings as they accumulate and you don't owe capital gains tax on profits when you sell investments in the account. As a result, your account has the potential to grow much larger than a taxable account with comparable earnings.

Based on your income you may qualify to deduct your contribution to a traditional IRA, or opt for a Roth IRA that can provide completely tax-free income in the future.

The ceiling for deducting your full contribution is scheduled to increase gradually to an adjusted gross income (AGI) of $50,000 for single taxpayers and $80,000 for married taxpayers filing a joint return. For 2001, the limits are $33,000 and $53,000.

To be eligible to put your total contribution into a Roth IRA, your AGI must be no more than $95,000 if you're single or $150,000 if you're married and file a joint federal tax return. You can make a partial Roth contribution if your income is between $95,000 and $110,000 if you're single and between $150,000 and $160,000

INVESTMENT COMPARISONS

TAXABLE VS TAX DEFERRED

TAXABLE	TAX DEFERRED
Advantages	**Advantages**
● Tax on capital gains at rate lower than regular rate	● No tax on earnings until withdrawal
● No limit on purchases	● With 401(k), no tax on contributions until withdrawal
	● No capital gains tax on profits from trades within the account
Disadvantages	**Disadvantages**
● Tax as you earn	● Tax at regular rate at withdrawal
● Tax on capital gains	

if you're married and file a joint return. Married couples filing separate returns don't qualify for either alternative.

A SECOND PERSPECTIVE

If you have a spouse or partner with investment assets, you might want to look at both portfolios when you allocate your assets. For example, if your spouse has a defined benefit pension that will pay 30% to 50% or more of his or her final salary—a generous but not uncommon

percentage—that could provide a substantial amount of the income you need in retirement. Having that income frees each of you to put an even larger percentage of your 401(k) and your taxable investment portfolios in equities.

On the other hand, if the bulk of your 401(k) account is in stock of the company you work for, you may want to put more emphasis on tax-exempt fixed-income investments in your taxable accounts to add some diversification.

TAXABLE INVESTMENTS

When you compare investing in taxable accounts to investing in tax-deferred accounts, you might think first of the disadvantages. In the case of taxable accounts, you've already paid income tax on the amounts you invest, you pay income tax on any earnings your investments produce (even if you reinvest them), and you owe tax on any profit you realize from a trade.

But the rate at which long-term capital gains are taxed is lower than your regular tax rate, which may help soften the tax blow. And any investment you hold for at least five years before you sell is taxed at an even lower rate. There's no cap on the amount you can invest in a taxable account in any one year, and you can sell an investment without penalty whenever you need the money. So if you concentrate

on certain investments in your taxable accounts and on other types of investments in your tax-deferred accounts, you can take full advantage of what each opportunity has to offer.

One rule of taxable investing is to concentrate on long-term growth, preferably equities that pay no dividends. It often pays to hold on to these investments for the long haul, or at least as long as they remain promising. Remember, you owe no income tax on unrealized gains—no matter how big they are.

Similarly, you're better off keeping tax-exempt investments, such as municipal bonds and municipal bond funds, in an ordinary taxable account. Otherwise you'll end up owing tax on the interest you receive, since all earnings on tax-deferred accounts are taxed when you withdraw them.

401(k) Portability

In almost all cases, you can take it with you.

You're right to give your highest priority to the investments you make in your 401(k) plan. Those choices are key to how quickly and how large your retirement savings account can grow. But if you investigate the basics of how your plan works, you'll also have a sense of how certain plan features can work to your advantage.

MOVING ON

No matter how good your 401(k) plan is, the job that goes with it may not be perfect. Or it may not be interesting or lucrative enough to make you turn down a new employer's offer. In fact, you may change employers a half-dozen times—or more—during your career. On average, full-time workers in the US switch jobs eleven times before they're ready to retire.

Almost 70% of 401(k) participants who get distributions spend the money they've accumulated in their plan rather than rolling it over to an IRA or new employer's plan. While age doesn't seem to influence that decision, the size of the account does. The smaller it is, the more likely its owner is to spend the money. But if, just once in 30 years, you took $10,000 out of your 401(k) instead of rolling it over so it could continue to accumulate tax-deferred earnings at 8%, your retirement fund could end up more than $100,000 short.

The good news about changing jobs is that your 401(k) is **portable**, which means you can leave it behind or take the value of your contributions plus any earnings with you when you leave. You may be able to roll over your 401(k) to your new employer's plan, and you can always roll it over to an individual retirement account (IRA).

If your new employer doesn't offer a retirement plan—and a significant percentage of small and midsized companies may not—or doesn't allow money to be rolled over into the plan, you can still move the assets you've accumulated to an IRA so that they can continue to grow tax deferred.

Or, you could take an early withdrawal and pay the taxes and potential penalty that would be due—although most advisers argue that's not the best choice.

MOVED OUT

Sometimes you don't have any choice about leaving your job. Your employer may be reducing the entire workforce, or you might not have been right for the position. Whatever the reason, you don't lose the contributions you've made to a 401(k) or any earnings they've produced. By rolling your account over into an IRA, you preserve its tax-deferred status. And you may eventually be able to transfer your assets to a new employer's plan.

If you're faced with a temporary layoff rather than termination, the best move may be to wait. Even if you're not adding to your account, what's already there has the potential to increase in value. If you're rehired relatively quickly, you'll be in the right position to go on contributing. And since 401(k) rules are quite strict about what constitutes a termination, you may not be eligible for a distribution in any case.

HAVE PLAN, WON'T TRAVEL

The more closely tied a retirement plan is to the employer who offers it, the less portable it is. For example, if you're vested in a traditional defined benefit plan, which promises to pay you retirement income from your employer's pension fund, you'll collect eventually—but not until you reach retirement age, no matter how many years, or jobs, in the future that is.

Some employers offer a type of defined benefit plan called a cash balance plan. It's designed to provide the security of a pension plus the flexibility of a portable plan. If you're part of such a plan, your employer invests and manages a pension fund to be used to pay retiring workers. While you're part of the plan, there's a hypothetical account in your name, which grows at a predetermined rate each year. If you leave your job, you can take the accumulated value of that account with you. But nothing is perfect: These plans are widely criticized as less generous for long-time employees than traditional plans.

IF YOU CAN'T WORK

If you're disabled during your working life, you may have the additional burden of demonstrating to your employer's satisfaction that your disability is severe enough to be considered a qualifying disability. If you meet that test, and if your plan provides for disability payouts, you have the same rights to the assets in your account as if you had reached retirement age. Taxes will be due on amounts you withdraw, but there's no early withdrawal penalty even if you're younger than 59½.

But qualifying can be difficult, especially if your plan uses the stringent Social Security guidelines. For example, if you can do any job you have the skills to do, even if you can't do the job you held before you became disabled, your employer may not consider you disabled. If that's the case, and you don't want to work at the job you're assigned, it can be considered the equivalent of quitting.

While nobody wants to anticipate a serious disability, it pays to know what your employer's policy on disability is. That includes asking about your eligibility for hardship withdrawals if you can't work.

I can't work

Look Before You Leap

Before you move a 401(k), tread carefully. There are rules that can trip you up.

If you leave your job for any reason before you're ready to retire, you'll have to decide how to handle your vested account balance in your 401(k) plan.

Each choice has some advantages and some long-term consequences. You have to choose carefully, because once you've made your decision, you can't change your mind.

But you do get a second chance as long as you keep your 401(k) assets in a tax-deferred account. That's because you'll have the same options if you switch jobs again. For example, if you move the account value to a new employer's plan and then change jobs again, you can move the entire accumulation, including any assets you previously rolled over from a rollover IRA or another employer's 401(k) plan.

TAKE IT OR LEAVE IT?

The first decision you need to make is whether to keep your assets in retirement savings or take them as cash. The immediate advantages of keeping your assets tax deferred are that you continue to postpone paying income tax on the principal and earnings, and you avoid a potential 10% penalty on any amount that you take. And in the long term, you improve your chances of having enough money to live on in retirement.

On the other hand, if you want or need the cash immediately, you can get it without a hassle when you leave your job, minus 20% witholding. All you have to do is ask your plan administrator for a check. You might treat the cash as a bonus, providing money to pay your bills, invest, or spend on a vacation.

But the IRS considers the payout an early distribution. Depending on your tax rate, you could owe 50% or even more of your account value in combined federal, state, and local taxes,

Roll over the money to your new employer's plan

Arrange a direct rollover to an IRA

Move the money into a rollover IRA yourself

Leave the money in your former employer's plan

Take the cash value of your account

401(k)

FINANCIAL

plus the 10% penalty. In the highest brackets, a $100,000 account could be reduced to $40,000 in cash after paying $50,000 in combined taxes and a $10,000 penalty.

The tax and penalty on your early distribution are due by the day your taxes are due, usually April 15 of the year following the year in which you received the money.

What's more worrisome about taking the money is that you'll have to start from ground zero to build your retirement savings. Once money loses its tax-deferred status, it can't be tax-deferred again. So even if you could afford to put back every penny you took, you wouldn't be allowed to do it.

The smaller your account value, the more tempting it can be to take the cash. Most people who make that choice have just a few thousand dollars invested. But if you liquidate your retirement savings three or four times during the early years of your career, what seems like a series of relatively modest withdrawals effectively wipes out what could have been the backbone of a substantial retirement account.

LET IT BE—FOR NOW

Sometimes the easiest thing to do when you change jobs is to leave your 401(k) account in your former employer's plan. If the investments the plan offers have been providing strong returns and the fees are reasonable, your savings may do as well there as anywhere else, at least for the time being. And leaving the account where it is takes one more load off your mind as you begin a new job or look for work.

Of course, since you won't be working at your old job anymore, you won't be able to make additional contributions to the account, and you won't qualify for matching contributions. In addition, some plans won't let you change

your asset allocation if you're not an active employee. But any earnings that your existing investments produce will increase the value of your account. And if you want to move the account at some point in the future to a new plan or a rollover IRA, you'll be able to do so. The one thing you don't want to do is to forget you've left it behind.

BE PREPARED

Planning to leave your 401(k) account in your old employer's plan may have one drawback. Some plans may charge higher fees if you're not an active employee to cover added recordkeeping costs. These extra fees may simply be a not-so-subtle hint to take your money with you.

But more significantly, if the balance in your account is $5,000 or less, you may be out of luck if you want to leave it behind. The government allows employers to cash out small accounts. If your account value is under $5,000 and you don't make your own arrangements for moving the money, you can expect to get a check for the account value minus 20% required withholding.

You can get caught if you don't realize that you not only have to set up an IRA to get a direct rollover from your old plan, but that you also must fill out the paperwork your former employer gives you within 30 days of receiving it. However, some employers don't enforce this rule and allow you to leave your account open. If you're vulnerable to being cashed out, it's worth investigating your employer's policy.

NEW EMPLOYER

New Job, New Plan

There can be advantages to having all your retirement savings in one account.

If you're changing jobs and your new employer offers a 401(k), sometimes the smartest move is to transfer your assets from your old employer's plan into the new one. That gives you a bigger base on which any new earnings can accumulate, and it means you have to keep track of just one set of performance reports.

Keep in old 401(k) plan?

Old 401(k) Plan

NEW JOB →

NOT YOUR CALL

You may or may not be allowed to roll your eligible assets into the plan at your new job. The law doesn't require it, so it's your employer's call.

In some cases, even when rollovers are allowed, you have to wait until you're eligible to participate. That might be as long as a year, as employers can set that as a minimum period for joining their plan. Other employers, though, let you roll over your vested assets at the time you take the job or at the next enrollment date. It's something you'll want to ask about.

Remember that the only way you can be cashed out of a plan once you join is if your account is worth $5,000 or less. If you're concerned about being forced out of a plan, rolling over assets from a former plan may be a relatively easy way to make sure you have enough to avoid being cashed out in the future.

MAKING THE RIGHT MOVES

If your new employer's plan allows rollovers, should you make the move? The answer depends entirely on the quality of the new 401(k) plan.

When you're eligible to participate in a self-directed plan, the only way to handle investment options that don't satisfy you is to avoid them and focus on other choices when you allocate your contributions. And your only recourse if the fees seem too high is to contribute less and look for other investment alternatives. You face the same choices each time you're eligible for a new employer's plan.

But when you have the option of moving existing assets into that new plan, it pays to do a thorough analysis before you decide. Obviously the more choices the plan offers, and the more of those that are strong-performing funds, the more likely it is that you'll find investments you're happy with.

If you're not satisfied with the choices, however, you'll have much more freedom to make better selections if you keep your money in a rollover IRA. Or you can simply leave the money in your old employer's plan, as long as you're permitted to do so. You can initiate a move at any time, not just at the time you actually change jobs.

ROLLOVER OR TRANSFER

You may hear the words rollover and transfer used to describe what happens when you move retirement money to an IRA or another 401(k). There is a difference between them, though the terms aren't always used precisely.

Rollover is the broader term. It means moving assets from one investment to another. For example, if you change jobs, you may be able to roll over your vested 401(k) plan assets from your old employer's plan to your new employer's plan. Or you can roll over those assets to an IRA. You may also be able to roll over a conduit IRA into a 401(k) plan.

A transfer is a rollover that's handled electronically, so that the assets are moved directly from one plan to another or from one IRA custodian to another.

SIGNING ON TO A NEW PLAN

To move money to your new employer's plan:

1 Make the necessary arrangements with the 401(k) plan administrator at your new job. With some plans, you have to select the investments you want to make with the lump sum you're moving into the account. In other situations, you may be able to transfer the whole amount to a money market account and allocate the money to individual investments gradually.

2 Get any required distribution forms from your current administrator and provide the details of your new plan.

3 Ask that a check be sent directly to the administrator of the new plan or, if the process is handled electronically, that the account value be transmitted directly to the new administrator.

INDIRECTLY DIRECT

It's okay if your former employer gives you a check for the value of your account rather than sending it directly to the new plan administrator. But it should be made out to the new plan administrator, not to you. All you have to do is turn it over within 60 days. If you do that as soon as you receive it, no time will be lost in putting your money back to work.

TRANSFER RIGHTS

If you're leaving a job where you've been enrolled in a 401(k) plan, the law says your plan administrator has to tell you in writing about the choices you have for handling the assets in your account. And you must have at least 30 days to make up your mind—though you don't have to take that long if you don't want to.

Specifically, your plan administrator has to tell you that you can roll over your account without owing any tax if you do it directly, and that nothing will be withheld. You should also be notified that you don't have to pay tax on any amount you roll over to a new plan or IRA within 60 days.

You should also be told all the other distribution options, including the fact that you may choose to roll over part of the value of your account and leave the rest in your existing account.

Setting Up a Rollover IRA

A rollover IRA is in a class act by itself.

If you're leaving your job and don't know what to do about your 401(k), you may want to choose a rollover IRA. It's the one alternative that's always available if you want to keep your assets and any future earnings tax deferred. A rollover IRA also offers you the most flexibility in choosing investments. And it gives you the most control over withdrawals when you're ready to start using the money.

To start the rollover process, you generally fill out an application provided by the financial institution to which you plan to transfer your money. You'll get a new account number, which you'll need to complete the rollover request form provided by your old plan administrator.

When you turn in the form, the administrator liquidates your assets and transfers the cash value to your rollover IRA, either electronically or by check.

Rollover IRAs have some unique qualities. You can move any amount into your account, provided you're moving it from an employer sponsored retirement plan. In addition, you're not limited to the $2,000 annual ceiling on traditional and Roth IRA contributions.

And you may be able to move money out of a rollover IRA into a new employer's plan without owing any income tax or penalty if the new plan accepts rollovers and you've kept the money that qualifies for such a rollover in a separate IRA.

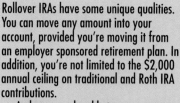

Rolling over keeps your earnings tax deferred

THE IRA ADVANTAGE
A rollover IRA shares the advantages of a traditional IRA. Your principal and any earnings accumulate tax deferred, which means your account value can grow more quickly than a taxable account with the same rate of return. And you have a wide choice of IRA providers and investments, whether you prefer insured bank accounts, mutual funds, individual stocks and bonds, or riskier choices such as futures and options. In fact, about the only investments you can't make are coins, artwork, and other collectibles.

Unlike employer plans, which normally allow you to begin withdrawing only after you retire, you can begin taking money out of an IRA without penalty when you turn 59½, even if you're still working.

And you can postpone withdrawals until April 1 of the year after you turn 70½. With some employer plans, you're required to begin taking retirement income when you retire. But with 401(k)s and other salary reduction plans, you have the option of rolling over the balance into an IRA to postpone withdrawals until 70½.

IRA CUSTODIANS

The financial institution where you open your rollover IRA is known as the custodian of your account. As custodian, the institution is responsible for making the investments you authorize, keeping track of the paperwork, and reporting investment performance and account balances.

But because most IRAs are self-directed, the custodian doesn't make investment decisions on your behalf. Nor does it have fiduciary responsibility for the way your investments perform. That means if you decide to put all your money into a risky investment, your IRA custodian isn't responsible for advising against it. The same is true if you keep all your money in a low-interest savings account.

Your custodian may charge an annual fee for handling your account—often as little as $10 a year, and rarely more than $50. And if your account balance reaches a certain amount, which the custodian sets, the annual fee may be dropped.

ROLLING DOWN THE FEES

Though you might not choose an IRA just to save money on fees, lower administrative cost is often a bonus of rolling over your 401(k). While there are sales charges on certain transactions, such as commissions on stocks you buy or sell, or management fees on mutual funds, there aren't additional fees based on the market value of your account.

> A rollover IRA gives you flexibility, a range of investment choices, and control!

PLAY BY THE RULES

You've got lots of leeway with a rollover IRA, but there are still some rules you have to follow.

Most importantly, you have to keep the rollover money separate if you ever plan to roll it over to a new employer's retirement savings plan. The best approach is to set up a new account for the rollover—which you may hear described as a holding account or a **conduit IRA**—rather than adding the money to an existing IRA account. You can't make contributions into this conduit IRA except for rollovers from a qualified plan, though you can use the conduit account to hold more than one rollover.

You can roll over your pretax contributions, your employer's matching contributions, and any earnings in your 401(k) or other qualified retirement account. But, if you've made any aftertax contributions to your plan, you'll have to take that amount as a cash distribution. You can't roll it over.

ONE AT A TIME

Keeping money in a rollover IRA isn't a long-term commitment, even if saving for retirement is. You can use a rollover IRA for a brief period between jobs, until you qualify for a new employer's plan, or for as long as you're satisfied with the investments you can make through the account.

If you never move your conduit IRA into a new employer's plan, nothing is lost by having kept it separate. It works the same way as any other IRA.

Indirect Rollovers

Moving your 401(k) on your own exposes you to hazards.

When you leave your job, you can ask your 401(k) plan administrator to write you a check for some or all of the value of your account. You then have 60 days from the day you receive the check to deposit the money in your new employer's plan or in a rollover IRA. When the money goes into the new account, it is still tax deferred, and so are any earnings the account generates in the future.

THROUGH YOUR HANDS

This method, known as an indirect rollover, can be appealing since it gives you short-term use of your money. The cash could come in handy, for example, if you have a contract to sell your home but it won't close for a couple of weeks and you need cash to close on your new one. In that case, you can use the money and still be fairly confident that you'll have it back in time to comply with the 60-day rule. But spending cash from your 401(k) on speculative investments is significantly more risky, since you can't be confident that you'll have the money when the deposit is due.

You may also choose an indirect rollover because you want time to decide where to reinvest, especially if you change jobs quickly or if you're looking for a new job.

But most experts fear it's too easy to put the decision off and risk missing the 60-day deadline. It's probably safer to do a direct rollover to an IRA money market account and then take as much time as you like to choose your long-term investments.

THE 20% PROBLEM

When you cash out of your 401(k), be prepared for an unpleasant surprise. The check you receive for the value of your account will be 20% less than you expected. That's because the IRS requires your employer to withhold that percentage to prepay some of the federal income tax you'll owe if you end up keeping the money instead of putting it back into a tax-deferred account.

For example, if you have $100,000 in your account, you'll receive a check for $80,000. You'll be entitled to get the $20,000 back once you file your tax return for the year, but only if you've completed a rollover within the 60-day period. If you miss the rollover deadline, you have to apply the 20% that was withheld against the federal tax you'll owe on the withdrawal. And, if you're under age 59½, you'll have to pay a 10% federal penalty on the total value of your account, plus state and local income taxes if you pay those taxes on other income.

60 DAYS

401(k)

U.S.S. ROLLOVER

20%

TAX BITE

There's another advantage of a direct rollover over an indirect rollover, which you handle yourself. You can do an indirect rollover only once each calendar year. If you try again, you'll have to pay taxes and penalties on the rollover amount. But you can do as many direct rollovers as you like.

Captain's Log
Day 40 of 60:
Rollover journey almost over. 401(k) earnings have proved useful for purchase of my new vessel. Not able to receive payment from selling my old boat yesterday. But despite my success and comfort in knowing I can use this money for a rollover IRA, there's still the 20% loss to taxes. Also worried about running into rough waters. If we don't reach land in 60 days, I will have another 10% penalty to face.

There's also a potentially bigger problem, one that simply keeping your eye on the calendar won't solve. When you open your rollover IRA, you'll have to come up with the 20% that was withheld—$20,000 in this example—from another source, such as your own savings, in order to deposit the full value of your account within the 60-day window. If you deposit just the amount you actually received, the IRS considers the 20% that has been withheld to be an early withdrawal.

That means you'll owe tax and, if you're not yet 59½, the 10% penalty on the missing 20% even though you never got the money. When you file your tax return, you'll get back the balance of the 20% that you don't owe in tax. But of course it will be less than the amount that was withheld.

To make matters worse, since what remains of the 20% that was withheld is considered an early distribution, it's no longer tax deferred. And you can't ever put it into an IRA or new employer's plan.

ESCAPING THE 20% WITHHOLDING

There are legal ways to get around having 20% withheld from your retirement savings plan distribution if you're leaving your job and need cash.

Perhaps the simplest is to arrange a direct rollover to an IRA and then do a second, indirect, rollover to another IRA. That gives you use of the money for 60 days.

STOCK ROUNDUP

To give you a check for the cash value of your 401(k), your plan administrator sells the investments in your account. But if some of your 401(k) portfolio is invested in shares of your employer's stock, you may be able to take the shares rather than having them sold. You can either put the shares in your rollover IRA or sell them and deposit the amount you get from the sale.

What you can't do is keep the stock and substitute an equivalent amount of cash to complete the rollover. And if you receive both cash and stock and roll over just part of the total value, you'll probably need to consult a tax adviser to be sure you report what you've done correctly on your tax return.

401(k) Loans

If you need cash, you may be tempted to raid your retirement savings. But plan to pay it back.

If you're like most people, there will be times when you need to borrow money. If your 401(k) plan allows loans—and many plans do—you might consider borrowing from your retirement savings. The approach is appealing. You usually don't have to explain why you need the money or justify how you spend it. The interest you pay goes into your account, not to some other lender. But taking a loan isn't as simple as just writing yourself a check.

Instead, you sign a loan agreement, just as you would if you were borrowing from another source. It will specify the amount you borrow, the term of the loan, the interest rate, any fees, and other terms that apply. And you may have to wait while your application is processed.

PAYBACK TIME
Most 401(k) loan agreements give you up to five years to repay. That's the longest period the government generally

When You Have to Borrow

Federal law **caps**, or limits, the amount you can borrow from your 401(k) at $50,000, or half the amount you have vested in the plan, or $10,000, if half the value of your account is less than that.

For example, if you have $150,000 vested, half is $75,000. You can borrow up to $50,000, because it's the smaller amount. But if you have $90,000 vested, half is $45,000. In that case, you'd be able to borrow up to $45,000.

There's sometimes a **loan floor**, or minimum amount you must borrow to get

a loan. For example, your employer may have a minimum of $1,000.

PAYING THE PIPER
Your plan won't give you—or anyone else, including the boss—a sweetheart deal on the interest rate you pay for borrowing against your 401(k). Rather, you'll pay a rate that's in line with what you'd pay on other secured loans. Many plans charge one or two percentage points above the current prime rate, the rate lenders set to reflect the cost at which they can borrow money themselves and still make a profit when they lend that money to consumers.

For example, if the prime rate is 8%, you may have to pay 9% to 10% interest on your loan. Loan rates are typically fixed for the term of the loan, but you may have the choice of a variable rate, especially if you're using a longer-term loan to buy a home. The advantage of a fixed rate is that you always know what your payment will be, which helps you budget for the cost. The advantage of a variable rate, on the other hand, is that if the prime rate drops, the interest rate you're paying will drop as well.

FEE FOR ALL
In addition to the interest you pay on a 401(k) loan, you may also have to pay a fee to arrange the loan and cover the cost of

WHAT YOU CAN BORROW

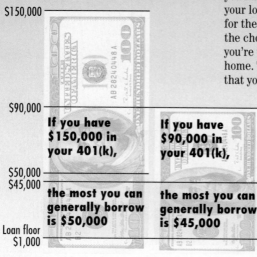

$150,000

$90,000

If you have $150,000 in your 401(k),

If you have $90,000 in your 401(k),

$50,000
$45,000

the most you can generally borrow is $50,000

the most you can generally borrow is $45,000

Loan floor
$1,000

allows. If you want to borrow for a shorter time, you usually can. And, in most cases, you'll probably be able to pay off your loan early if you want to.

There's one exception to the five-year rule. If you're using the loan to buy a primary residence—the home where you and your family will live—some plans give you 25 years to repay. This exception doesn't work for buying a vacation house.

A SECOND TIME AROUND

If you're repaying a 401(k) loan, or if you've finished repaying one during the past 12 months, you'll have to do a little more calculation to figure out what you can borrow on a new loan. You'll need to know your highest loan balance, or the most you owed in the past 12 months, as well as what your loan cap is.

To find your new maximum, subtract your highest loan balance from your loan cap. For example, if the balance in the past year peaked at $8,500, and half your

vested amount is $45,000, the maximum you can take as a new loan is $36,500.

SPOUSAL CONSENT

Some plans require you to get your spouse's approval before you borrow from your 401(k). Consent is essential in any plan that requires a joint and survivor lifetime payout provision, which means retirement income is paid over both lifetimes. Other types of plans may require spousal approval as well.

If you're separating or getting divorced, spousal consent for a loan can become a serious point of controversy. Your spouse might have a right to a portion of your 401(k) assets—or you may have a similar claim on your spouse's assets. If one of you borrows from your own account, and then changes jobs and doesn't repay, the other spouse's rightful share could be affected. You might want to consult an attorney if you anticipate a potential problem.

---

the required paperwork. Each plan sets its own fees, so you'll need to check with your plan administrator. You may also want to compare the fees to what you'd pay another lender for processing your application.

Loan fees may be figured as a percentage—perhaps 0.5%—of the loan amount or, in some cases, as a percentage of the balance in your account.

While 0.5% sounds rather modest, it can add up, especially if it's based on the account balance. For example, suppose you have $500,000 in your 401(k). The most you can borrow is $50,000. If the 0.5% fee is figured on $500,000, you'll pay $2,500 to arrange your loan. That's 5% of the amount you actually borrow.

LOAN FEES CAN SNEAK UP ON YOU

$500,000

If you have $500,000 in your 401(k),

$50,000

and you borrow $50,000...

$2,500

LOAN FEE 0.5% OF TOTAL

5% OF BORROWED

you owe 0.5% of the total, but that is 5% of the borrowed amount, or $2,500

Two Faces of 401(k) Loans

There are advantages—and some serious drawbacks—to borrowing from your 401(k).

Before you borrow from your 401(k), ask yourself a hard question: Is this really a good financial move? True, there may seem to be an advantage to borrowing from yourself—or, more precisely, your vested retirement account—because you're paying yourself the interest on your loan. In reality, however, taking a 401(k) loan is more complex—and more fraught with problems.

GOING TO THE WELL

When you take a loan from your 401(k), the money usually comes out of the investments you have in the plan. So if you have assets in four mutual funds, the money will come from one or more of those funds.

In many plans you may not have a choice of which funds to borrow from. Your employer may determine which investments the loan comes from, either by having you take money out of all of them proportionally—25% from each of four investments, for example—or by designating the one or ones from which the loan money will come.

In a few plans, you may be able to say which investments you want to borrow from. The advantage of being able to choose is that you can leave the investments that are providing the strongest returns untouched and borrow from the others.

For example, if you have some money in stock funds and some in fixed-income funds, you might choose to borrow from the fixed-income funds and leave the stock funds intact. However, you may have allocated the smallest portion of your contribution to fixed-income investments and they may have also increased the least in value. That might mean you still have to borrow from your stock funds to get the amount you need.

In Your Best Interest

The interest you pay on a 401(k) loan typically goes back into your account along with your principal. So if you're paying yourself 9% interest on $50,000 over five years, you add $12,275 to your account during that period.

At first glance, that seems like a great idea. And in some cases it may be. For example, if you took the loan from stock funds in your account during a long stock market slump, when the value

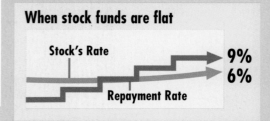

When stock funds are flat

Stock's Rate

Repayment Rate

9%
6%

PUTTING MONEY BACK TO WORK

Loan money you repay is reinvested. But how and when that reinvestment happens varies from plan to plan. It's one of the things you should check as part of making a decision about whether to borrow.

Many plans reinvest as you repay, dividing the amount among the various investments you've chosen in the same proportions as your pretax contribution. For example, if your contribution is

Loan Type A

Reinvested as you pay

LOAN

YOUR PLAN

HOW REPAYMENT WORKS

In most cases, you begin to repay a 401(k) immediately after getting a check for the amount of the loan. The principal and interest you repay may be credited directly back to your account, or it may be credited to an account your employer has set up to collect repayments from everyone in the organization who has taken a loan. If the money is funneled through a repayment fund, your account will be credited with your principal and interest or with your principal and your share of the blended interest the fund earns on all the loans being repaid.

of your account was flat or didn't increase much, the interest could provide a boost. But in a period of strong stock market growth, equity mutual funds may produce annual returns of 15%, 20%, or even higher.

If you've borrowed money during a time like that, you've shortchanged yourself twice. To begin with, the money you've borrowed isn't invested, so it can't be earning strong returns. In addition, you're repaying at a lower rate than the funds' potential earnings, which also represents a loss of earnings.

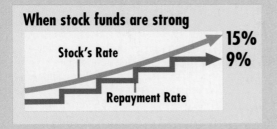

When stock funds are strong

Stock's Rate — 15%
9%
Repayment Rate

spread equally among four funds, your repayment would be reinvested that way as well.

But plans that create a loan fund to receive your payments and the payments of other borrowers may hold all of your repaid principal and interest in that fund until you've paid off everything you owe. At that point, the lump sum is allocated among your investments. If that's the case, the earning potential of your investments may be less than what it might have been if money was reinvested as you repaid it.

Loan Type B

Reinvest from loan fund

LOAN FUND
$
LOAN
YOUR PLAN

CHECK THE RATES

Depending on your access to credit from other sources, you could end up paying a lower interest rate on a loan from your 401(k) than you'd pay for a personal loan from a bank or other commercial lender.

And you're almost certain to pay a lower rate than you would if you charged the expense to a credit card—if your credit line is even large enough to let you borrow the amount you need.

But there are other ways to borrow that could cost you less than borrowing from a 401(k) loan. If you own your home, for example, you might consider taking a home equity loan. There are risks to this strategy, however, since you could lose your home if you default on the loan. But the rates are often about what you would pay on a 401(k) loan, and the interest is generally tax deductible.

You might also think about refinancing your mortgage for a higher amount. Or, if you're a member of a credit union or eligible to join one, you might investigate what it would cost to borrow from there. You may find it's cheaper than borrowing from a commercial lender such as a bank, and less complicated than taking a 401(k) loan.

The Great Loan Debate

It pays to consider both sides of a 401(k) loan.

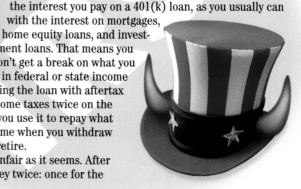

There are potential tax consequences from taking a 401(k) loan. The good news is that you don't owe income tax on the amount of the loan as long as you pay it back. In fact, that's one of the strongest reasons for borrowing from your account rather than withdrawing the amount you need from your IRA or applying for a hardship withdrawal from your 401(k).

On the other hand, you can't take a tax deduction for the interest you pay on a 401(k) loan, as you usually can with the interest on mortgages, home equity loans, and investment loans. That means you don't get a break on what you owe in federal or state income taxes. And since you're repaying the loan with aftertax money, you end up paying income taxes twice on the same amount—once before you use it to repay what you borrowed and a second time when you withdraw the money, usually after you retire.

But that might not be as unfair as it seems. After all, you're also using the money twice: once for the loan and once for retirement.

DOUBLE WHAMMY

With most plans, you repay your loan through payroll deductions. Your employer withholds the amount that's due from your paycheck, usually once a month. A few plans require you to repay by personal check, and some others allow that method if you prefer.

Because your loan repayment is deducted from your paycheck, it might feel the same as making a contribution. But it's not, even though money is going into your account. Repayments just return money that was already in the account. To keep your account growing, you've got to add regular contributions as well.

In fact, the danger with having loan repayments deducted is that you may be tempted to stop contributing to your 401(k) while you're repaying your loan, feeling you're stretching yourself too thin. According to one study, approximately half the people who borrow from their 401(k)s reduce their contributions while they repay, and some stop contributing entirely.

That's a double whammy. You'd be paying back old contributions at 8% or 9%, and missing out on possibly higher earnings if the money had remained invested. And you'd be missing out entirely on the tax deductibility and earnings potential of new contributions.

PRETAX vs. AFTERTAX DOLLARS

There's a crucial difference between making a pretax contribution and repaying a loan with aftertax dollars. Suppose, for example, your gross income is $500 a week, you contribute 10% of your pretax income to your 401(k), and 30% of your income is withheld for taxes. Your take-home pay would be $315.

$	500	Gross weekly salary
−	50	Contribution to 401(k)
= $	450	Pretax income
−	135	30% withholding
= $	**315**	**Take-home pay**

But instead of contributing $50 to your plan, suppose you have to use that money to repay $50 on your 401(k) loan.

$	500	Gross weekly salary
−	150	30% withholding
= $	350	Aftertax income
−	50	Repayment of loan
= $	**300**	**Take-home pay**

Your loan repayment won't necessarily be as high as 10% of your gross salary. But the example illustrates that when you use aftertax dollars to repay your 401(k) loan, your take-home salary goes down while your taxes go up.

FEELING THE PINCH

If you leave your job, you'll probably have to repay your entire loan balance within 30 to 90 days of your departure. If you don't repay, you're in default, and the remaining loan balance becomes a withdrawal. That means you owe income tax on it. And if you're younger than 59½, you'll owe a 10% federal penalty in addition to the tax that's due.

It's extremely unusual to be able to transfer a loan to a new employer's plan, though it's probably worth asking about, especially if you've been recruited to the new position. Or you may be able to arrange a personal loan, called a floater loan, or advance against your salary or bonus to settle your debt.

The repayment, tax, and penalty rules generally apply even if you've been laid off and you're unemployed. Unless you can borrow the amount you owe, you'll have to

A COSTLY DEPARTURE

It's probably not a good idea to borrow from your 401(k) if:

- There's a chance you'll lose your job
- You're planning to leave your job
- You're nearing retirement

Remember, you have to pay back the loan shortly after your employment ends. If you can't, the tax and potential penalty could make your departure a costly one. And, if you have an outstanding loan balance when you retire, you can't roll it over to an IRA.

deal with the IRS. But that isn't because your employer is hard-hearted. There's little flexibility in the regulations that govern loans from 401(k) plans. Your employer risks having the entire plan declared ineligible for not abiding by the rules.

When you're considering a loan from your 401(k), it's smart to check out what works for and against you

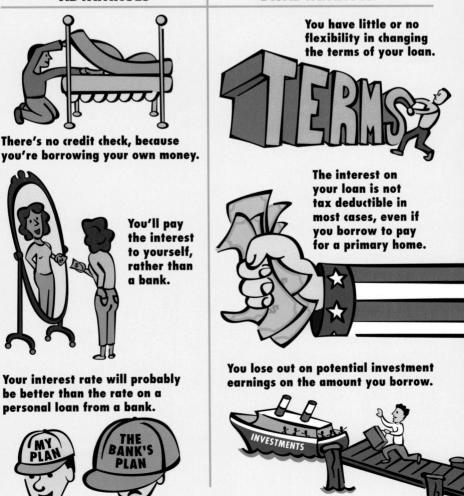

ADVANTAGES

There's no credit check, because you're borrowing your own money.

You'll pay the interest to yourself, rather than a bank.

Your interest rate will probably be better than the rate on a personal loan from a bank.

MY PLAN

THE BANK'S PLAN

DISADVANTAGES

You have little or no flexibility in changing the terms of your loan.

TERMS

The interest on your loan is not tax deductible in most cases, even if you borrow to pay for a primary home.

You lose out on potential investment earnings on the amount you borrow.

INVESTMENTS

Hardship Withdrawals

Withdrawing from your 401(k) plan to handle hard times can be hard work.

In a financial emergency, your 401(k) plan might seem like the best place to turn, especially if you've saved a substantial amount for retirement. But it's rarely the best choice unless you're older than 59½. If you're younger, you may find that your plan won't let you make what's known as a **hardship withdrawal** at all. And even if your plan allows these early withdrawals, you may find that they're hardly worth the trouble.

The first complication is that every plan requires you to pass a rigorous test to determine whether your situation even qualifies as a hardship. Beyond that, you have to show you can't reasonably get the money you need any other way.

SPONSOR'S CHOICE
Employers who sponsor 401(k) plans may allow hardship withdrawals, but they aren't required to. Those who make hardship withdrawals available may believe that you'll be more likely to contribute to the plan if you know you'll have access to your money if you really need it.

PLENTY OF RED TAPE

Any request for a hardship withdrawal will definitely result in lots of paperwork.

To begin with, your 401(k) plan administrator will almost surely want proof of how much money you need, such as itemized medical bills or a mortgage statement showing how much you are behind.

With supporting documents, you can withdraw money to cover a documented bill, plus enough to pay the taxes that will be due on the total withdrawal. But you can't withdraw more than you can prove you need. And if you end up not spending the entire amount you withdraw, you can't use any part of it to open a rollover IRA or other tax-deferred account.

With certain hardship withdrawals, you must also be able to prove that you don't have any other resources readily available to meet your financial emergency. For example, if you have $40,000 in unreimbursed medical expenses, that's considered an immediate and heavy financial need that would qualify as a hardship. But if you have $60,000 in a money market fund or US Treasury bills, you can't take a hardship withdrawal to cover the $40,000 bill.

ALL MONEY IS NOT EQUAL
Even if you do qualify for a hardship withdrawal, you can't use all of the money in your 401(k) account.

What's an Emergency?
There are a limited number of financial circumstances that the IRS—and therefore your plan, which must follow IRS rules—recognizes as a financial hardship. The rules permit withdrawals only to:

Cover out-of-pocket medical expenses for you or a dependent

Keep from being evicted from your home, or having your mortgage foreclosed

In most cases, you can withdraw money that you contributed yourself, but you can't withdraw your employer's matching contribution or any earnings on those contributions, even if you're vested.

Suppose the total value of your 401(k) is $193,000, of which you contributed $50,000. Generally, the total you could take as a hardship withdrawal would be $50,000.

The one exception is that plans that existed before 1989 may include all your pretax contributions and earnings credited through December 31, 1988, in the amount you can take as a hardship withdrawal.

NO STONES UNTURNED

To make sure that you don't have any other money available, some plans will ask you to sign a statement saying you can't get the money any other way. You're generally expected to affirm that you have:

- Been turned down for insurance coverage, if insurance applies
- Spent any available cash and liquidated your assets (though not your home or car)
- Withdrawn any aftertax dollars you contributed to your 401(k) account

- Borrowed the maximum from your 401(k) and from commercial lenders

Other plans consider you eligible if you have taken all the loans and other distributions you're eligible for from your employer's plans. But if you qualify this way, you're not allowed to make contributions to a 401(k) or other employer sponsored plan for at least 12 months after you take the withdrawal.

FOLLOW-UP HEADACHES

If your application is approved, your plan administrator will send a Form 1099-R to the IRS, reporting the amount of your hardship withdrawal. The tax on this amount will be due when you file your return for the year, but you may have to make estimated tax payments so that the amount you owe on April 15 isn't more than the maximum acceptable amount, typically $500.

Your plan administrator may follow up after the withdrawal as well to see if you used the withdrawal to pay for your hardship.

Put a downpayment on a primary home

Pay college tuition for you or a dependent if the tuition is due in the next 12 months

Your 401(k) plan might allow for additional hardship withdrawals if they are in the spirit of the IRS rules. For example, you may be able withdraw money to:

Pay funeral expenses for a close relative

Repair damage to your home that's not covered by insurance

One bright spot is that your application won't be rejected on the grounds that you knew or should have known the expense was coming and didn't make other plans to pay for it.

Going to the Well

When you withdraw you have to take enough to cover the tax that's due.

Every time you withdraw pretax money from your 401(k), you owe income tax. A hardship withdrawal is no exception. And if you're younger than 59½ when you withdraw, you generally owe a 10% penalty as well. You may escape penalty if you have to cover medical expenses that exceed 7.5% of your adjusted gross income and aren't covered by insurance.

REQUIRED WITHHOLDING

Your 401(k) plan automatically withholds 20% of what you withdraw. So if you need $40,000, you'll have to request a withdrawal of at least $50,000 to end up with the amount you need.

You can apply the amount that's withheld to your tax bill when you file your return. But it's unlikely that 20% of your withdrawal will be enough to cover what you owe, especially since the amount you take is added to your other income and may boost you into a higher tax bracket.

One solution is to ask that more be withheld. The drawback, of course, is that the more you have withheld, the more you have to withdraw to get the money you need to handle the hardship—and the higher your tax bill and any potential penalty will be.

PRETAX WITHDRAWAL

A NOTE FROM HOME
Your 401(k) plan may also require your spouse to agree in writing to any hardship withdrawal.

Income tax due on earnings

10% penalty for withdrawal before age 59½

IRA

401(k)

TIMING A HARDSHIP WITHDRAWAL

Chances are, tax planning is the last thing you'll be thinking about when you're considering a hardship withdrawal. But if you can put off taking the money from the end of one tax year until the beginning of the next, you add a year to the time that taxes and potential penalties on the withdrawal are due.

For example, if you take the withdrawal on January 2 instead of December 28, you have 15 months to pay the tax instead of three months. Of course, the 20% that's withheld from your withdrawal will be in the government's hands longer, but you'll have more time to get the additional tax you owe together.

A December 28 withdrawal gives you only 3 months to pay taxes

A January 2 withdrawal gives you 15 months to pay taxes

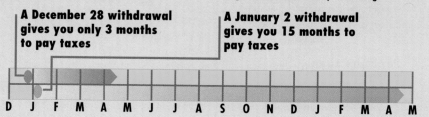

D J F M A M J J A S O N D J F M A M

THE REALLY HARD PART

Hardship withdrawals can create potential hardships of their own.

The biggest problem is often the tax bite. If your combined federal, state, and local income tax rate is 40%, and you owe a 10% penalty, you'll have to use half of any withdrawal to meet those obligations or you'll risk a problem with the IRS.

If you have already borrowed the maximum from your 401(k) to qualify for the hardship withdrawal, you could be as much as $50,000 in debt. That would mean repaying $10,000 plus interest to your 401(k) every year for five years on top of your other financial obligations.

Any money you withdraw also reduces your potential retirement savings in two ways: That amount won't be available in the future, and it won't produce any earnings to help your account grow.

Automatic 20% withheld

10% penalty for early withdrawal that doesn't qualify for exception

In addition, for 12 months after you take a hardship withdrawal, you may not be able to contribute to your 401(k) plan. When that year is up, the law says you'll be able to make only limited contributions for the remainder of the calendar year.

While this restriction may seem insignificant when you need the money, it will keep you from rebuilding your retirement assets quickly after your financial situation gets resolved.

HITTING THE IRA TILL

The rules for withdrawing from your individual retirement account (IRA) are different from the rules for a 401(k) plan. You can't borrow from your IRA as you may be able to from your 401(k). But you may have an easier time getting the money out of your IRA before you turn 59½.

With a traditional IRA, you can take an early withdrawal without the 10% penalty for several specific reasons, including using the money to pay college tuition, cover medical expenses, or make a downpayment of up to $10,000 on a first home for yourself, your children, your grandchildren, or your parents. Income taxes are due on the earnings portion of your withdrawal and on the entire withdrawal if you deducted your contributions when

you filed your tax returns. But unlike a 401(k), you can start rebuilding your account as soon as you're financially able.

With a Roth IRA, you can withdraw your contributions at any time without owing income tax on the amount you take out. And you can withdraw earnings on those contributions without penalty if you're disabled, are paying medical expenses, or using up to $10,000 for a first-home downpayment. But you will have to pay taxes on the earnings.

There are a few drawbacks to IRA withdrawals. Any money you take out of your IRA is no longer able to produce earnings, which undercuts your long-term savings plans. And you'll probably have to withdraw enough to pay the income tax that's due as well as the amount you need for a specific expense. For example, if you need $10,000 and you're in the 28% federal tax bracket, you'll have to withdraw closer to $13,000 to have enough to pay tax that's due. And if your state imposes tax on investment earnings, you'll have to plan for that amount too.

DO IT RIGHT

Before you take money out of an IRA, check with your tax adviser to be sure your reason for withdrawal fits the guidelines. Owing a 10% penalty on top of the tax that's due on your withdrawal can mean you end up short of the amount you need.

Legal Problems

Your 401(k) can end up in a legal crossfire.

If you owe money to people, businesses, or governments, you've got creditors who want you to pay up. They might even take you to court to try to force you to liquidate your assets to settle your debts. But whether or not your creditors can get at your 401(k) depends on who they are and what legal route they take.

DEALING WITH DEBTS

If you have commercial debts—that is, you owe money to a business, such as a roofing company, or a professional, such as your lawyer—those creditors can sue you in federal or state court to collect your debts.

FAMILY MATTERS

If you get divorced, your former spouse may be entitled to some of the value of your 401(k), or to a portion of the plan itself. What happens depends on where you live.

In community property states (Arizona, California, Idaho, Louisiana, Nevada, New Mexico, Texas, Washington, and Wisconsin), you and your former spouse will generally divide the value of the 401(k) accounts that you own at the time of your divorce equally. In the other states, the standard is equitable distribution. That means that while you and your former spouse divide the 401(k) assets that accumulated during your marriage, it may not be a 50/50 split.

A former spouse who is entitled to part of your 401(k) account can choose to:
- Take the money in cash
- Roll the money over into an individual retirement account (IRA)
- Leave the money in the 401(k)

DIVIDING A 401(k) IN A DIVORCE
Each of the choices has some advantages and some potential drawbacks.

	ADVANTAGES	DISADVANTAGES
Take a cash distribution of account value	• No 10% penalty, even if you and your former spouse are both under 59½	• Income taxes are due on the amount you withdraw • If your former spouse gets the cash, your former spouse pays • If your children or other dependents get the cash, you pay • The tax-deferred status of the money is lost
Choose a rollover IRA	• No income taxes • No 10% penalty • More investment options than with a 401(k) • Tax-deferred status continues	• Available only to former spouses • Not available to children and other dependents
Leave the money in the 401(k) plan	• No income taxes • No 10% penalty • This is the only tax-deferred option available to children and other dependents	• Arrangement might get complicated • Fewer investment options than for rollover IRA

If they sue in federal court, your 401(k) is safe. A federal court will **not**:

- Order you or your 401(k) plan administrator to take money out of your account to pay your creditors now
- Freeze your 401(k) until you pay your debts
- Reserve any part of the money in your 401(k) to pay your debts years from now when you withdraw money

If your creditors sue you in state court, however, they might try to collect from your 401(k), or ask the court to earmark some of your assets to pay your creditors whenever you withdraw money. However, ERISA law, which governs 401(k)s, supersedes state law in these cases.

But if you owe money to family members or the federal government, a court can order you to withdraw money from your 401(k) to pay those debts. That includes money you owe for child support, alimony, and taxes you owe to the IRS. But state and local taxing authorities can't get at your 401(k) assets for money you owe them.

KEEPING THE LID ON

Because your 401(k) is safe from debt collection, don't let anyone, including your lawyer, pressure you into agreeing to withdraw money from your 401(k) to pay debts or let you volunteer to do it.

At certain crossroads—including changing jobs or retiring—you'll have the option of taking your money out of your 401(k) in a lump sum or rolling it over to an IRA. If you do, the money will no longer be protected from creditors in federal or state courts.

If you have large debts, you might consider leaving your 401(k) in your employer's plan if that's possible.

IN OVER YOUR HEAD

If you're deeply in debt, you can file for personal bankruptcy, which lets you reorganize your finances. Some of your assets are used to pay some of your debts while other assets are protected.

One problem with declaring bankruptcy is that you may put your IRA but not your 401(k) up for grabs. That's because even though you file for bankruptcy in federal court under federal law, the federal bankruptcy law looks to your home state's laws to determine which of your assets are protected. If the state where you live considers IRA assets available for debt payment, you may lose these assets to your creditors. So before you make a final decision, you may want to consult a bankruptcy lawyer who can tell you whether your savings will be at risk.

SPLITTING UP

To get a share of your 401(k), your former spouse's attorney will ask the court to issue a Qualified Domestic Relations Order (QDRO). The QDRO instructs your 401(k) administrator to divide your account assets between you and your former spouse by creating two subaccounts, one that you control, and one that your former spouse controls. In effect, each of you becomes a participant in the 401(k) plan, with the same rights as other participants.

Once a QDRO is issued, your plan administrator has 18 months to rule on its validity. Your former spouse's attorney may ask that the assets be frozen so that you can't borrow them, withdraw them, or roll them into an IRA before the order is accepted as qualified.

Required Withdrawals

Sooner or later you'll have to withdraw—and later is better.

While you're contributing to your 401(k), the focus is on building your account—choosing investments, keeping track of performance, and making changes to your portfolio. Eventually, you or your beneficiary will reap the long-term rewards of participating in a retirement savings plan. But to get the benefits, you must abide by the rules for taking the money out.

OPTIONAL, THEN REQUIRED

From the day you turn 59½, you can start taking money out of your 401(k) if your plan allows it. But if you don't need the money, you don't have to take anything out. In fact, you can go on contributing if you're working. If you're retired at 65, you must begin taking your benefit unless your plan allows you to defer until you turn 70½. And if you're retired by the time you turn 70½, or you're a 5% owner when you reach that age, withdrawals become mandatory. By April 1 of the year after you turn 70½, officially known as your required beginning date, you must set up a withdrawal schedule and take the first of your **minimum required distributions**. Each year from that point on you take another distribution.

ARE YOU 70 OR 71?

The first step in figuring your required distribution is finding your life expectancy. To do that, you use your age, or how old you are. But that's trickier than it sounds.

Here's why: You have to begin required distributions for the year you turn 70½. Whether you're considered 70 or 71 when you're 70½ depends on your birthday.

If you were born between January 1 and June 30, you turn 70½ in the same calendar year that you are 70. So you use 70 to determine your life expectancy. But if you were born between July 1 and December 31, you turn 70½ in the following calendar year, when you'll also turn 71. So you use 71 to determine your life expectancy.

STRETCH IT OUT

The larger your account, generally the more you must withdraw each year. For example, if your account value is $600,000 and your life expectancy is 16 years—as it is when you're 70—your required minimum distribution would be $37,500 for the year. But if your account value is $1 million, your required minimum would be $62,500.

DISTRIBUTION OR WITHDRAWAL

The money you take from your 401(k) is officially described as a **distribution**, though in practice it's often called a **withdrawal.**

When your plan handles the paperwork and makes a series of automatic payments to your bank account, it's easy to see how it's a distribution. But when you roll over your 401(k) to an individual retirement account (IRA), it's your responsibility to figure out how much you must take each year. And you must be sure you actually take it. That may seem much more like a withdrawal.

THE TEN YEAR RULE

To find joint life expectancy, you use your age and your beneficiary's age.

But there's an important catch to increasing your life expectancy, called the **minimum distribution incidental benefit (MDIB)** rule. If your beneficiary is anyone except your spouse, you must

But the longer your life expectancy, the smaller your required distribution must be. If your life expectancy is 26.2 rather than 16 years, you would have to take $22,901 from an account worth $600,000. From an account worth $1 million, you would have to take $38,168—roughly 40% less in each case.

If you want to extend your life expectancy, there's an easy way to do it. You choose a beneficiary. If you don't name a beneficiary, or if you name your estate, a charity, or other institution, your life expectancy depends on your age alone. If you name a beneficiary, your life expectancy depends on two ages—yours and the beneficiary's. That's known as a joint life expectancy, and it's always longer than single.

MAKING MATH SIMPLER

The instructions for figuring your **minimum required distribution** say to multiply your account value times a fraction with 1 as the nominator and your life expectancy as the denominator. That looks like this: $600,000 x $\frac{1}{16}$. What that actually means, in practical terms, is dividing the account value by your life expectancy, or $600,000 ÷ 16.

$$\frac{\text{Account value}}{\text{Life expectancy}} = \text{MRD}$$

your life expectancy

Without a beneficiary

	Age	Life expectancy
You	70	16 years

Account value = $600,000

$$\frac{\$600,000}{16} = \$38,168 \text{ MRD}$$

With a beneficiary

	Age	Joint life expectancy
You	70	26.2 years
Beneficiary	60	

$$\frac{\$600,000}{26.2} = \$22,901 \text{ MRD}$$

calculate your joint life expectancy as if that person were no more than ten years younger than you.

For example, if you're 70 and your 35-year-old daughter is your beneficiary, your joint life expectancy would be 47.5 years according to the IRS tables. But following the MDIB rule, your life expectancy is actually 26.2—as if your daughter were 60. The rule was almost certainly written to prevent you from minimizing distributions during your lifetime by choosing a much younger beneficiary, in effect using your retirement savings plan as a tool to build your estate.

In contrast, you can use your spouse's actual age to calculate joint life expectancy, even if there's more than a ten-year age difference. The younger he or she is, the longer your joint life expectancy will be.

PENALTY PHASE

You can take more than your required distribution. In fact, the IRS will probably be happy that you're paying the income tax that's due sooner rather than later. But if you take less than is required, or if you forget to withdraw before the end of the year, you face a 50% federal income tax penalty on the amount you should have taken but didn't.

For example, if your required distribution was $18,000 but you took only $10,000, you'd owe $4,000 in penalty (half of the $8,000 difference between the required amount and your actual with- drawal) in addition to the regular tax due. There are rare occasions when the IRS will accept your explanation for taking too little and waive the penalty. But don't count on it.

PENALTY 50%

This Is Your Life Expectancy

You may have more than one life expectancy—though probably not nine.

Just as you can extend your life expectancy by naming a beneficiary, you may be able to stretch out the number of years the IRS allows you to take required withdrawals by choosing the way you calculate that life expectancy.

There are three methods: **term certain**, **recalculation**, and **hybrid**.

If you are using just one life, you may use the term certain or recalculation. If you name your spouse as beneficiary, you may be able to use any one of the three. And if you name anyone but your spouse you may be able to use term certain or hybrid.

TERM CERTAIN

The most straightforward method of calculating joint life expectancy is **term certain**—sometimes also called joint term certain, fixed term, or period certain.

Here's how it works: In the year you're ready to begin receiving distributions, you look up your joint life expectancy using the tables in IRS Publication 590. If you've named a beneficiary and that beneficiary is 69, your joint life expectancy is 21.1 years. The next year, you subtract one year from the joint life expectancy you used the previous year. In this example, that would be 20.1 years.

As each year goes by, you subtract one from your life expectancy, dividing your account balance by a smaller number. In this example, it would be 19.1 in the third year, 18.1 in the fourth year, and so on. Using this method, in theory at least, your 401(k) will be empty at the end of the term certain, or 21.1 years after you began taking money out.

Using this method, the amount you withdraw should be approximately the same each year as the year before, not taking potential investment earnings or losses into account.

JOINT RECALCULATION

A second method of calculating life expectancy, called **joint recalculation**, is a little more complicated. Rather than figuring out your life expectancy just once and reducing it by one each year, you use the IRS tables each year to find your new life expectancy.

Surprisingly, it changes. That's because the longer you live, the longer you can expect to live, or so the statistics show.

Here's how recalculation works: Suppose you're 70 and your spouse is 69. The IRS says your joint life expectancy is 21.1 years. Now jump ahead five years, when you're 75 and your spouse 74.

COMPARING JOINT LIFE EXPECTANCIES

	TERM CERTAIN				JOINT RECALCULATION		
	Spouse's Age	Your Age	Joint Life Expectancy		Spouse's Age	Your Age	Joint Life Expectancy
DISTRIBUTION BEGINS	69	70	21.1		69	70	21.1
YEAR 2	Subtract **1** each year. No need to look up age in IRS tables.		20.1		70	71	20.2
YEAR 3			19.1		71	72	19.4
YEAR 4			18.1		72	73	18.5
YEAR 5			17.1		73	74	17.7
YEAR 6			16.1		74	75	16.9
YEAR 11			**11.1**		79	80	**13.2**

If you were using the term certain method, you would have subtracted five from 21.1, because five years have gone by. Your joint life expectancy would then be 16.1 years. But under the recalculation method, the joint life expectancy of a 75 year old and a 74 year old is 16.9 years. In other words, instead of losing a full year of life expectancy each year, you lose only part of a year.

The difference between the two methods becomes even greater after 10 years. Using the term certain method, your joint life expectancy would be 11.1 years when you were 80 and your beneficiary 79. But under the joint recalculation method, it would be 13.2 years.

However, once you make the decision to recalculate, you must do it every year.

HYBRID

The **hybrid** method of calculating life expectancy, sometimes known as the split method, allows either you or your beneficiary to use the term certain method to determine life expectancy, and the other to use recalculation. In other words, one of you determines your single life expectancy before the first 410(k) distribution and subtracts one year from that number each year. The other uses the IRS table to recalculate life expectancy every year.

It doesn't matter which of you uses the term certain method and which of you recalculates.

The rub is that the hybrid method requires a more complicated calculation each year than looking up numbers in a table or doing simple subtraction. Briefly, you must determine what's known as the **adjusted age**—rather than the actual age—of the partner who is using the term certain method. Then that partner uses the adjusted age to find a new single life expectancy, which you use to find your joint life expectancy.

But don't throw up your hands. The math isn't hard. And your plan administrator should be able to refer you to a software program or online calculator to do the work for you.

HYBRID MATH

You can follow these steps to calculate joint life expectancy using the hybrid method for determining minimum required withdrawals.

1. Start with the actual age of the person using the period certain method and look up the single life expectancy of this person in the year withdrawals begin.
2. The next year, subtract one year from that life expectancy.
3. Then work backwards, looking up the age in the single life expectancy table that corresponds to the new life expectancy. That gives you the adjusted age.
4. Use that adjusted age and the actual age of the person who is recalculating to determine the new joint life expectancy by looking it up in the joint life expectancy table.

APPENDIX E. (Continued)

DIVISOR		TABLE II (Joint Life and Last Survivor Expectancy					
AGES	35	36	37	38	39	40	41
65	47.7	46.8	45.9	44.9	44.0	43.1	42.2
	47.7	46.7	45.8	44.9	44.0	43.1	42.2

APPENDIX E. Life Expectancy Tables

AGE	DIVISOR	TABLE I (Single Life Expectancy)*		AGE	DIVISOR
60	24.2				
61	23.3				
62	22.5			98	3.0
63	21.6			99	2.8
64	20.8			100	2.7
65	20.0			101	2.5
66	19.2			102	2.3
67	18.4			103	2.1
68	17.6			104	1.9
69	16.8			105	1.8
70	16.0			106	
71					

HYBRID

	Spouse using term certain			Spouse using joint recalculation	
DISTRIBUTION	Age	Single Life Expectancy	Adjusted Age	Age	Joint Life Expectancy
BEGINS	69	16.8	69	70	21.1
YEAR 2	70	15.8	71	71	19.4
YEAR 3	71	14.8	72	72	18.9
YEAR 4	72	13.8	74	73	17.7
YEAR 5	73	12.8	75	74	16.9
YEAR 6	74	11.8	77	75	15.8
YEAR 11	79	10	79	80	**13.2**

A Closer Look

Life expectancy is part understanding the numbers,
part weighing the odds.

What makes choosing among the methods
for calculating life expectancy complicated is that the method that can result in
the smallest distributions—recalculation—is effective only if you or both you
and your spouse live a long time. And
there's the problem: You can predict life
expectancy, but you can't count on it.

LONGER TERM, BIGGER BITE
Using the recalculation method can
reduce your required distribution because
your life expectancy actually increases as
you live longer. That allows you to divide
your account bal-
ance by a larger
number than you
can using the term
certain method,
resulting in smaller
required distributions
over a longer time.

Once you choose to recal-
culate, however, you must use
that method every year. While you
and your spouse are alive, you use the
joint life expectancy tables. When one
of you dies, the remaining partner
recalculates based on his or her single
life expectancy.

For example, if you're 70 and your
spouse is 65 when you begin required
withdrawals, your joint life expectancy
according to IRS tables is 23.1 years. If
your account is valued at $600,000, your
first distribution would be $25,974. But if
your spouse dies during the year, your life
expectancy drops to 15.3 years when you
recalculate your next distribution.

Assume your account has accumulated
earnings at 8% at the time of its final
valuation for the year, and is worth
$619,948. Dividing that amount by 15.3
would make your required distribution
$40,519—a substantial jump over the
$25,974 you took the previous year. The

result would be an increase in your
income taxes and a big dent in
your account.

A CERTAIN APPEAL
If you use the term certain method, your
joint life expectancy drops a bit faster
while you are both alive than it does if
you recalculate. But if you or your spouse
dies, the surviving spouse can continue to
withdraw at the same rate as if both of
you were alive.

For example, if you are 70, your spouse
is 65, and your account value is $600,000,
your first withdrawal would be $25,974,
based on a life expectancy of 23.1 years.
That's the same amount as a recalculation withdrawal. But assume your
account increases 8% in
value during the next
year, to $619,052,
and your spouse
dies that year, just
as in the previous
example. Your sec-
ond-year withdrawal
using term certain
would be $28,052 ($619,948 ÷ 22.1 =
$28,052)—which is significantly less
than the $40,519 you would have to
withdraw with recalculation.

BY DEFAULT
If you don't choose a method for calculating
life expectancy, the default provision of
your plan determines the method. If your
plan doesn't have such a provision, then the
IRS rule of single life expectancy takes effect. But remember that some plans
require you to choose a specific method.
You should be sure to find out what flexibility you have.

THE HYBRID GAME
The appeal of the hybrid method of
figuring life expectancy—when one of
you recalculates and the other uses term
certain—is the opportunity to hedge your
bets. While you're both alive, you may be
able to withdraw a smaller amount each
year than if you'd used a straight term
certain approach, although not as little
as if you were using joint recalculation.
And, if you guess right which spouse will

A WORD OF WARNING
Many defined contribution plans offer a
limited number of distribution options
and may not pay distributions over a life
expectancy. Many beneficiaries, whether
your spouse or not, take your death benefit
as a lump sum distribution.

Using certain term		Using joint recalculation	
You are 70 and your spouse is 65			
$600,000	Account balance	**$600,000**	Account balance
÷ **23.1**	Life expectancy	÷ **23.1**	Life expectancy
= **$ 25,974**	Required withdrawal	= **$ 25,974**	Required withdrawal
You turn 71 after your spouse dies			
$619,948	Account balance	**$619,948**	Account balance
÷ **22.1**	Life expectancy	÷ **15.3**	Life expectancy
= **$ 28,052**	Required withdrawal	= **$ 40,519**	Required withdrawal

IN THE BALANCE

You'll want to weigh the pros and cons before you decide how to calculate life expectancy.

Calculation method	Advantages	Disadvantages
Term certain	Original withdrawal schedule applies, even if you or your beneficiary dies Contingent beneficiary can withdraw on same schedule	If you outlive your life expectancy, you could drain your 401(k) before you die
Joint recalculation	Smallest annual withdrawal while you and your spouse are both alive	No contingent beneficiary allowed, as withdrawals end at death of second spouse If either of you dies, the other's minimum withdrawals increase
Hybrid	More potential protection against depleting your 410(k) before you die than with term certain	Slightly larger minimum withdrawals than with joint recalculation Risk that survivor will have to use single life expectancy

die first, the surviving spouse will have the advantage using a term certain schedule to minimize withdrawals.

The catch—and it's a big one—is that if the person who is using the term certain method dies first, the person who is recalculating will have to use his or her single life expectancy to calculate future withdrawals, which will increase the required withdrawal amount, perhaps

dramatically. That's why financial planners often recommend that the younger spouse or the spouse in better health is the one to use the term certain.

However, there is an escape clause. The surviving spouse can always roll over the assets remaining in the 401(k) into an individual retirement account (IRA), choose a new beneficiary, and start a new—presumably longer—withdrawal schedule.

Choosing Your Spouse

The IRS gives its tax blessing when you name your spouse as your beneficiary.

If you're single, you can choose anyone you wish as beneficiary of your 401(k). But if you're married, your plan requires you to name your spouse as beneficiary, just as pension plans do. To name anyone else, you must have your spouse's written permission.

THE SPOUSE HAS IT

There are good reasons for your spouse to be your beneficiary. First, naming your spouse lets you provide for his or her long-term financial security, something that's likely to be high on your list of retirement goals. In addition, there are significant tax and long-term planning benefits that apply when you choose your spouse. You can think of these benefits as the government's way of approving your choice.

What's more, since the value of any assets that you pass directly to your spouse, or to a trust for your spouse's benefit, reduces the value of your estate, naming your spouse as your beneficiary can help reduce or eliminate the threat of estate taxes. That leaves more principal available to produce future income.

When someone other than your spouse is your beneficiary, the value of the account is included in the value of your estate. That may push the total over the point at which the estate becomes taxable—$675,000 in 2001, $700,000 in 2002 and 2003, and $1 million by 2006.

Of course, estate taxes could eventually be due if the value of your surviving spouse's estate, including your 401(k) assets, reached the taxable level. But as more time passes, and more money is withdrawn, the likelihood that the value of your 401(k) will make your estate subject to taxes also diminishes.

SPECIAL TREATMENT

A spouse who is the beneficiary of a 401(k) or other salary reduction plan has withdrawal options that other beneficiaries don't have.

For example, if you die before you begin to take money from your account, your spouse can postpone withdrawals until December 31 of the year when you would have turned 70½. However, a beneficiary who is not your spouse,

such as a grandchild, must start to withdraw by December 31 of the year following the year of your death, or must take everything out of the account by the end of the fifth year after the year of your death.

Your spouse can also roll over the value of the money in your 401(k) to an Indiv-idual Retirement Account (IRA) in his or her own name, designate a new beneficiary, and potentially create a new withdrawal schedule. Having an IRA also means greater choice of investments, since your spouse is no longer limited to the investments available through your plan. But a beneficiary who is not your spouse, such as your child, doesn't have the option of rolling over the assets to an IRA.

TIMING A ROLLOVER

Your surviving spouse can roll over your 401(k) assets into an IRA at any time after your death. And the rollover can be for either the total value of your account or for any part of it.

The only restrictions are those that apply to all IRA rollovers. Basically, that includes not being able to roll over any aftertax contributions you made to the plan or any amounts that you were required to take as a distribution. For example, if your required minimum distribution is $10,000 in the year you die, that amount can't be rolled over.

While it's never too late to do a rollover, there may be times when it's too soon. That could be the case if your spouse is younger than 59½ when you die, immediately rolls over your 401(k), and then needs to withdraw a lump-sum amount. That amount is ordinarily subject to the 10% early withdrawal penalty, unless the reason for the withdrawal, such as paying college tuition, makes it exempt from the penalty.

In contrast, if your surviving spouse had left the money in your 401(k), no penalty would apply to a lump-sum withdrawal. That's because the income from the 401(k) (or from an IRA in your name) is considered a **death benefit** and isn't subject to the penalty. In either case, though, the withdrawal is taxable income.

IT'S NOT A LOCK

The flexibility to change beneficiaries gives you a number of options for distributing your assets differently if your life situation changes. For example, if it becomes clear you're likely to die before you begin taking required withdrawals, you might consider naming a much younger beneficiary. That beneficiary will be able to calculate the required withdrawal amount each year based on his or her own life expectancy, rather than on the shorter period of the joint life expectancy of you and your spouse. That could mean stretching out the income over a very long time, allowing the bulk of the account to continue to accumulate tax-deferred earnings.

There are other good reasons to change beneficiaries. For example, if your spouse should die before you do, you'll need to name someone else to receive income from your 401(k) after your own death. The same may be true if you divorce, end a long-term relationship, or if it turns out that your original beneficiary doesn't need the money and someone else does.

Remember, though, that if your plan requires you to name your spouse as beneficiary, you'll need his or her permission to make a switch. Your plan administrator will probably have a standard signature form that you can use.

Other Beneficiaries

Just about the only 401(k) beneficiary you can't choose is the family pet.

Sometimes choosing a beneficiary who isn't your spouse makes good financial sense. While other beneficiaries can't postpone taking distributions or roll over your 401(k) into their own individual retirement accounts, they may receive income from your account for a long time—in some cases for decades.

DOUBLE VISION
You don't have to choose just one beneficiary. If you want two (or more) of your surviving children to share your account, for example, you can name them both, using wording that says explicitly if they are to share equally or in another proportions you prefer. Most experts advise allocating shares by percentage rather than dollar amounts, since there's no way to be certain what the account will be worth at your death.

You may want to consult a retirement planning specialist to discuss whether you should have separate accounts established—one for each of your beneficiaries—at the time of your death. The primary reason for separate accounts is that, if you haven't begun required with-

drawals, each beneficiary can use his or her own life expectancy to figure the size of the required distribution. That allows a younger beneficiary to withdraw smaller amounts over a longer period.

Another alternative, if you have more than one 401(k), a 401(k) and an IRA, or a 401(k) and another retirement savings plan, is to name separate beneficiaries for each plan. While the accounts may not all be the same size, you can always equalize your legacy in other ways.

CLASS ACTION
If you want to leave some of your 401(k) assets to your children or grandchildren, you can name an entire group, or what's known as a **class**, as your beneficiary. You don't have to list individuals by name. In fact, the size of the class might increase or decrease as more children are born, or if someone dies.

The only requirement for naming a class is that it has to be possible to determine the age of the oldest member, since that person's age determines the

50%

PICKING A TRUST
You may name an **irrevocable trust** or a **testamentary trust** that's established through your will as the beneficiary of your 401(k) plan. An irrevocable trust is one that you can't change once it's been set up, and a testamentary trust takes effect after your death.

Because the beneficiaries of the irrevocable trust are fixed, the age of the oldest beneficiary can be determined. Therefore, the period over which distributions must be made can also be calculated, as required by the plan. In contrast, you can't name a revocable trust

life expectancy of the class. Whether this choice makes sense for you depends on the size of your 401(k) account and the number of people in the class. You'll probably want to discuss this option with a financial adviser who specializes in retirement planning before you decide.

BENEFICIARY BACKUPS

When you designate a primary beneficiary, you should also choose a **contingent beneficiary** or beneficiaries. If the primary beneficiary dies or turns down the right to collect, the contingent beneficiary assumes that role.

For example, you might name your spouse and your daughter as primary and contingent beneficiaries. If you and your spouse were to die in an accident— or what's considered a simultaneous death—the value of your account would pass directly to your daughter.

TAKE A QTIP

You can also name a **qualified terminable interest property trust (QTIP)** as beneficiary of your plan. This type of trust benefits your spouse, though it gives the trustee the power to control how the distributions are made. The logic behind a QTIP is that you can designate what should happen to the assets in your 401(k) if your spouse remarries, becomes ill, or is inexperienced in handling financial matters.

While a QTIP has some of the advantages of naming your spouse as direct beneficiary, including postponing estate taxes, it has the potential drawback of increasing the required annual distribution. That could mean higher income taxes and a greater chance that your spouse could outlive your 401(k) assets.

NO PLACE FOR AN ESTATE

A number of experts suggest you think twice about naming your estate as your 401(k) beneficiary. That's because an estate is a legal entity and has no life expectancy. Your account

value would have to be liquidated, ending its tax-deferred status.

In addition, if it were liquidated within a single year, your estate might owe income tax at the highest marginal federal rate—39.6%—plus state and local taxes where they apply. That could reduce the amount your heirs ultimately receive.

as your 401(k) beneficiary because you have the right to change the ultimate beneficiaries of that type of trust as often as you choose. So it's not possible to fix the age of the oldest beneficiary or determine the term of the distribution.

One advantage of choosing a trust is flexibility in allocating distributions from the plan. For example, you might instruct the trustee to evaluate individual needs or levels of maturity in dividing up the amount that must be taken out of the plan each year. In contrast, if you named a class of beneficiaries, with each receiving a set percentage of the total annual distribution, those allocations are fixed even though the circumstances of the beneficiaries might change.

Switching Tactics

Timing matters if you plan to change your beneficiary.

Since you have the right to switch the beneficiary you've named for your 401(k) plan, it's smart to review your choice from time to time.

You should certainly take a second look when there's been a major alteration in your personal life, whether it's a happy event such as a marriage, or a distressing one, such as a death. Or, if you've named your two children as beneficiaries but one of them turns out to be financially comfortable and the other is struggling, you might want the needier one to have a source of regular income.

It's especially smart to evaluate your beneficiary decision before you begin to take **minimum required distributions (MRD)** after you reach 70½. After distributions begin, you don't have as much flexibility in making changes.

CHANGING BENEFICIARIES BEFORE DISTRIBUTIONS BEGIN

If you change your 401(k) beneficiary before you take your first required distribution, you may be able to accomplish several goals at once.

For example, if you change your beneficiary from your 70-year-old spouse to your 35-year-old son, you can extend the joint life expectancy you use to figure the mandatory withdrawal amount by up to ten years. That would mean you could take smaller distributions and owe less income tax each year. It should also help you extend the life of your account.

In addition, if you die before you begin to take the required distributions, your son can use his actual single life expectancy to find the amount of the annual distributions he's required to take. If he was 45 when you died, that could mean income based on a life expectancy of 37.7 years.

RESPONSE MECHANISMS

There are a number of other circumstances that may trigger a decision to change your beneficiary. For example, if your spouse is your beneficiary but is in poor health, and therefore unlikely to need the money, you might decide to substitute another person.

Similarly, if your spouse has a substantial retirement plan or has just received a

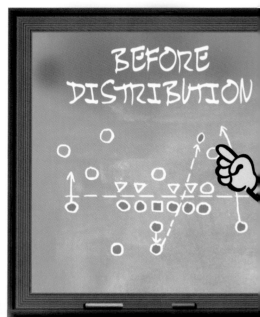

PAY ATTENTION
While you have the legal right to change beneficiaries after you begin mandatory withdrawals, some 401(k) plans may not allow changes after April 1 following the year you turn 70½. Check with your plan administrator. If there's a deadline for changes, you don't want to miss it.

large inheritance, you might decide to name a different beneficiary who needs the income more.

Remember, though, that you don't have to share the income you receive from your plan with your beneficiary while you're collecting it. The income goes to you while you're alive and to the beneficiary only after your death.

GET IT DOWN

If you do want to change your beneficiary, be sure you make it official by filing the form your plan administrator requires. You should get an official copy back to keep with the rest of your financial records.

TAKE A CLOSER LOOK

If you're going to change beneficiaries, it's often better to act sooner rather than later. If you wait until you've taken just one required distribution, any beneficiary but your spouse is locked into your withdrawal schedule. But if you switch before you start taking income, your beneficiary may be able to use his or her own life expectancy to calculate withdrawals after your death.

For example, if your daughter was 35 and you died at 70 before taking a distribution, she could calculate her minimum required distribution based on her life expectancy of 47.3 years.

AFTER DISTRIBUTIONS BEGIN

You can also change your beneficiary after you begin taking mandatory distributions. But your first withdrawal is a critical turning point because you can never use a longer life expectancy to calculate the required distribution than you use to calculate the amount you take the first year. (The only exception is if you switch to an older beneficiary. Then you must use your new, shorter, joint life expectancy.)

For example, if you change your beneficiary from your 70-year-old spouse to your 35-year-old son, you cannot reduce the amount of each future distribution. True, you can still accomplish the goal of having your son collect income after your death. But if you've already begun to take distributions—even if you've received only one—your son will have to withdraw using the same withdrawal schedule you had established using the joint life expectancy for you and your spouse.

DISTRIBUTIONS TO YOUR BENEFICIARIES

If you are 70 and your beneficiary is:	And you've taken one distribution, your beneficiary:	You die before taking a distribution, your beneficiary:
Your 45-year-old son	May figure life expectancy based on actual age and your age at time of death	May use life expectancy of 37.7 years to calculate withdrawals
Your 35-year-old daughter	May figure life expectancy based on actual age and your age at time of death	May use life expectancy of 47.3 years to calculate withdrawals
Your three nieces, ages 35, 32, and 30	May figure life expectancy based on actual age of eldest and your age at time of death	May share the distribution for a period of time, based on the life expectancy of the eldest
Your 69-year-old spouse	May take income on existing schedule or roll account over to IRA, naming new beneficiary	May postpone distribution or roll account over to IRA, naming new beneficiary

Finishing Touches

What you need with your 401(k) is a set of step-by-step instructions.

As simple as it is to put money into a 401(k), it's surprising how complicated it can be to take the money out. There are some rigid—even draconian—rules to follow, so you must be prepared to deal with them yourself, and be sure that your beneficiary or beneficiaries know about them as well. For example, your beneficiaries should know who they are, how to contact your plan administrator, and the essential rules for taking distributions. They should also know where to find copies of all your essential 401(k) or rollover IRA documents, including:

- The current beneficiary designation
- A statement signed or stamped by your plan administrator identifying the method you're using to calculate life expectancy if you've started to take distributions
- Your account records

ONE YEAR AT A TIME

Your 401(k) plan may be set up to pay your minimum required distribution on a regular schedule, typically monthly. If that's not the case, you must determine the amount and timing of your withdrawals. For example, you can withdraw the entire amount as early as January, once you can get the valuation for the previous year, or as late as December 31. You can take a fixed amount in monthly installments, or you can take the money as you need it.

But you have to be careful to take at least the minimum amount by the December 31 deadline. You can't postpone taking any part of your distribution into the next year. And, if you take more than the required amount one year, you can't use the excess to offset what you must take the next year.

(Illustration: a woman holding a book labeled "Instructions" standing over an open box labeled "401(k) PLAN" filled with dollar bills.)

TWO IN ONE

The first year you take distributions may be the hardest year to get things right. That's because if you wait until April 1 of the year following the year you turn 70½ to take your first required distribution, as the law allows, you'll have to take two distributions: one that's required for the year you're 70 (by April 1), and another required for the year you're 71 (by December 31). And don't forget, you'll owe the income tax that's due on both distributions in the same year.

TAX BITE

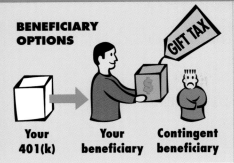

BENEFICIARY OPTIONS

GIFT TAX

Your 401(k) → Your beneficiary → Contingent beneficiary

I DISCLAIM

Your 401(k) → Your beneficiary → Contingent beneficiary

RESTAKING YOUR CLAIM

If your best laid plans turn out to be less than ideal, or if the beneficiary you've designated before you die isn't the best choice for estate-planning purposes, there may be a chance to amend your decision—though it's not something your beneficiaries should try to negotiate without legal advice.

For example, suppose you name your sister as beneficiary and her daughter as contingent beneficiary. If your sister has a generous retirement plan of her own, or has begun to collect on her husband's plan, she might want her daughter to benefit from your plan right away. But if she took a distribution from your plan and simply passed it along, not only would she owe income tax on the amount, but

she might also be faced with gift tax if the amount were over the tax-free limit—$10,000 in 2001.

Instead, your sister could **disclaim**, or refuse to accept, the designation as beneficiary and the income she would receive. In that case, the contingent beneficiary— her daughter—would become the primary beneficiary. Instead of making a gift, your sister is refusing to take one.

As always, there are rules to be aware of, including the rules of the state where the disclaimer is made. For example, the person who is disclaiming can't have taken any benefits, can't decide who the new beneficiary is, and must make the disclaimer within nine months of your death, which is not a lot of time where such matters are concerned.

THE YEAR OF THE BENEFICIARY

The same distribution rules that apply to you also apply to your beneficiary after you die. For example, if the plan pays your distributions, they'll be paid to your beneficiary. And if the plan allows flexible distributions, your beneficiary can take out the money on any schedule during the year, as long as he or she takes at least the required minimum before December 31 each year.

It's essential, though, that your beneficiary takes the first required distribution by December 31 of the year following the year of your death. If that date goes by, the opportunity to take distributions based on your joint life expectancy is lost for good, and the entire value of your 401(k) must be withdrawn by December 31 of the fifth year following the year you died.

If it's not certain that your designated beneficiary will qualify for distributions based on life expectancy, experts suggest that the person you've named begin taking money by the end of the first year after your death in order to preserve the right to an extended distribution schedule. Even if the IRS decides your beneficiary designation doesn't qualify for such a distribution schedule—as it may not if you've named both a person and a charity,

for example—the money will have to be withdrawn anyway.

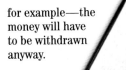

CITIZENSHIP ISSUES

If you're married to someone who isn't a US citizen and if your estate, including your 401(k) assets, is large enough to be vulnerable to federal estate taxes, you'll need professional advice if you want to name your spouse as beneficiary.

That's because assets left to a spouse who isn't a citizen don't qualify for the marital deduction. And using a **qualified domestic trust** (QDOT) to reduce estate taxes can jeopardize your spouse's ability to reduce income taxes over the long term.

What Beneficiaries Need To Know

It's not enough to name your beneficiaries. You need to educate them, too.

Naming a beneficiary is good for you, if what you want to do is extend the period over which you're entitled to withdraw from your 401(k) or from the IRA into which you've rolled over your account. And it can be a good deal for the beneficiary, too, as the value of your account may provide either a lump-sum windfall or a steady stream of income, potentially for decades.

But unless your beneficiary or beneficiaries know what decisions to make and the potential advantages and pitfalls of their choices, your desire to enrich someone you care about could be shortchanged (enriching Uncle Sam instead).

FLIGHT 401(K)

What your beneficiary needs:

1. A copy of your beneficiary designation
2. A copy of your death certificate

IT'S ALL IN THE PLAN

You should check with your 401(k) plan administrator about the choices your beneficiary has, as the details of one plan are likely to differ in certain ways from the details of another.

While it might not occur to you to worry about these issues while you're building your account, the unpleasant reality is that you could die unexpectedly. It's probably as important for your beneficiary to have a sense of how to handle financial decisions in such a circumstance as it is if you live to be 100.

You should review the choice again just before you begin taking your required distributions, since starting to take money out fixes the length of the payout and may have other consequences as well.

Your plan may not insist that your beneficiary make an immediate decision, about what to do at the time of your death, and may extend the deadline for six months or more. But the federal government imposes a schedule that can't be ignored without risking either a substantial penalty or the possibility of being locked into a course of action.

SHARING THE NEWS

If, when you die, your assets are still in 401(k), your beneficiary must notify your plan administrator, fill out a claim form, and submit the form with an official copy of your death certificate and a copy of your beneficiary designation. That presumes, of course, that the beneficiary knows who he or she is, who the plan administrator is, and where to find a copy of the beneficiary designation. That's the information you must provide.

If you've worked with a retirement benefits adviser or an estate attorney, that person should have copies of the documents your beneficiary needs. In that case, be sure your beneficiary knows whom to call. You may even want to introduce your beneficiary to your adviser to make it easier for them to interact. If you haven't worked with a professional, you may want to create a file with the documents your beneficiary will need.

Notification can be more complex if you have several plans. And there's always the risk that money you put into an earlier plan will be abandoned if your beneficiary doesn't know where to look. That's one of the strong arguments for consolidating your retirement accounts, either with your current employer or in an IRA.

WHAT THE CHOICES ARE

If your beneficiary is someone other than your spouse, he or she has two choices:

 Take a lump sum distribution

2 Receive an annual income

3 If your beneficiary is your spouse, there's a third alternative: rolling over the assets into an IRA in his or her own name.

LUMP-SUM ISSUES

On the plus side, taking a lump sum can provide an immediate cash infusion that might make it easier to buy a home, send a child to college, build a business, or whatever is important to the recipient. On the down side, the amount that's actually available will be diminished, potentially substantially, by the income taxes that are due. That's one of the big reasons your beneficiary should think twice about withdrawing to reinvest.

However, your beneficiary should know that, if you were born before 1936 and would have been entitled to use ten-year

forward averaging to calculate the tax, he or she can use that method as well. If that's the case, it's smart to consult a tax expert before making any final decisions.

CARRYING ON

To preserve the right to a stream of income from your plan, your beneficiary must take the first distribution by December 31 of the year following the year of your death. For example, if you died in 2001, your beneficiary would have to take a distribution by December 31, 2002. That keeps everything on schedule, since the distribution for the year you die is taxable as income to you.

If the beneficiary misses the deadline, nothing happens right away. But overnight the rules change. Now there is no alternative but to withdraw every penny in the account by December 31 of the fifth year following the year of your death. Using the same example, that would mean December 31, 2006. Your beneficiary could withdraw before that date, but would risk a 50% penalty on the amount that should have been withdrawn but wasn't. How big is that? It's huge.

Suppose your 401(k) account was worth $500,000, which your beneficiary was supposed to withdraw. Missing the deadline would mean forfeiting $250,000 right off the top.

Your beneficiary could lose half...

for not withdrawing on time.

Deciding the Future

A 401(k) isn't a game, but it does have rules—and ways to come out ahead.

Flexibility is one of a 401(k)'s greatest charms. When you retire, you can leave your account where it is, in your former employer's plan. You can pack up your assets—figuratively speaking—and roll them into an IRA. Or you can take some or all of the your assets in cash and spend the money as you please.

You can start taking money from your account without penalty any time after you turn 59½, or you can leave it alone until you turn 70½ (or sometimes even later if you're still working). You can continue to make investment decisions for your account assets, or you can leave things as they are.

But precisely because you have so many choices, you and your beneficiaries may be short-changed if you don't put time and effort into planning how and when to take money out of your 401(k).

STRIKING A BALANCE

One of the biggest challenges may be how to use your 401(k) plan effectively to meet as many of your financial goals as you can.

Some of those goals are likely to have a direct impact on your own well-being, such as being sure you'll have a source of income for as long as you live, and minimizing the amount you owe in income taxes each year. You may also want to provide long-term financial support for your spouse or partner, or set aside assets for your children or grandchildren to inherit. Or you may want to make charitable gifts to organizations or institutions that are important to you.

But some unexpected conflicts may add a level of complexity to your planning. For example, in reducing your withdrawals to minimize the income tax you owe, you run the potential risk of increasing the taxes that may be due on your estate. Estate tax rates start at 37% and increase rapidly to 55%—in contrast to a top income tax rate of 39.6%.

ALL IN THE NUMBERS

Despite the potential for estate taxes, there's a lot to be said for minimizing the amount you withdraw in any year. Perhaps most important, more of your assets can grow tax deferred for a longer period, which helps reduce the possibility of outliving your resources.

If you're not convinced that holding onto your retirement account's tax-deferred status makes more sense than taking money out to reinvest on your own, consider this example.

If you withdraw $10,000 from your 401(k) account and pay 28% in income tax, you'll have $7,200 to invest. That amount, invested for ten years, would be worth $12,605 if your return was 8% and you paid tax on the earnings each year at the 28% rate.

But if you left the $10,000 in your 401(k) account or rolled that amount into an IRA, it would be worth $21,589 after ten years with an 8% return. If you withdrew that amount and paid tax at 28%, you'd still put $15,544 in your

Please wait for your distribution!

Finish

Congratulations! You will receive a payout of $15,544.

LEAVE IT IN YOUR 401(k)

$10,000	Tax-deferred amount invested
$21,589	10 years at 8% earnings
x .28	Income tax rate
$15,544	Your amount
	You'll have **$2,939** more

pocket (or your bank account). That $2,939 difference is what tax deferral is all about. And, the longer the period over which the money stays invested, the larger the difference grows. After 20 years, your $10,000 would be worth $46,610 and after 30 years, $100,630.

Sorry! Pay 25% income tax and have less to invest.

Withdraw some money now

You owe estate tax of up to 50%!

You

Start

Leave money in 401(k)

TAKE IT OUT

$10,000	Withdrawal	
x .28	Income tax rate	
$7,200	Amount invested for 10 years at 8% earnings	
$12,605	Your amount	

TIMING ISSUES

Taking money out of your 401(k) isn't hard. But it's not like getting money from your bank. You can't walk up to a teller and leave with a check—whether you're taking a lump sum, rolling your account over to an IRA, or beginning to take annual distributions.

There are two reasons. First, your account has to be valued to determine how much it is worth. Every 401(k) plan values each employee's account on a regular schedule, from as often as daily to weekly or monthly, or as infrequently as quarterly. But no plan does a separate valuation of individual plans because the account holders want to move their money or start distributions. For example, if your application for a withdrawal or rollover is filed just after your plan's quarterly valuation, you'll have to wait until the next one. In addition, 401(k) plans may keep your money for up to 60 days after valuing your assets. They don't have to wait the maximum time, of course, but they have the right to do so. Again, you should expect to wait. Planning can prevent the potential time lag from becoming a problem, whether you're trying to take required distributions on time or need to tap other sources of income while you wait for your first retirement savings check. In many cases, the administrator will take the initiative, alerting you that it's time to make a decision and preparing you for how long it will take to start receiving income. But the bottom line is that it's your responsibility to meet the distribution deadlines.

On another front, if you're doing a rollover, ask your 401(k) administrator how often the plan values its assets, and how long it will take for the money to show up in your new account. If nothing else, knowing how long you can expect to wait can keep you from worrying that you've made a mistake in initiating the transfer.

Strategic Planning

The more sources of retirement income you have, the easier it is to manage your finances.

With a traditional defined benefit pension—if you have one—you generally begin receiving a fixed income when you retire. The amount you receive is based on the terms of your employer's plan. In most cases, you can't postpone the payments even if you don't need the money to live on.

Social Security works essentially the same way as a pension: A predetermined amount is paid on a fixed monthly schedule over your lifetime and the lifetime of your surviving spouse, if you're married. The only difference is that you can choose when to start receiving Social Security income—from as early as 62 until you turn 70, when the annual bonus you get for postponing benefits stops increasing.

WHY WAIT?

If you've retired, there's usually little motive for postponing Social Security income past your full retirement age—65 if you were born through 1937, increasing gradually to 66 and then to 67 for people born from 1955 on. Statistically you're likely to collect more of the benefit you're entitled to if you start collecting sooner. And you're free to do whatever you want with the income, including investing it. The only reason to wait is that up to 85% of your Social Security benefit is taxable at your regular federal income tax rate if your income is more than $34,000 if you're single, or more than $44,000 if you're married.

ON YOUR TERMS

Unlike a pension or Social Security, which provide a fixed amount on a fixed schedule, you may be able to influence the timing and the amount of income you take from a 401(k). More important, if you make the right decisions at the right time, you can extend the life of your assets for decades beyond your death to provide a combination of tax-deferred growth and regular income for your spouse, children, or grandchildren.

If the money in your 401(k) is your primary source of retirement income, you can begin withdrawing when you retire, rather than asking your employer to postpone distributions. Then when you reach 70½, the amount you must take is based on what's left in your account.

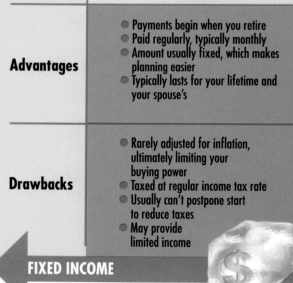

Each type of retirement income

While you can never have too much retirement income, you have to learn how to manage different sources.

PENSION

	PENSION
Advantages	● Payments begin when you retire ● Paid regularly, typically monthly ● Amount usually fixed, which makes planning easier ● Typically lasts for your lifetime and your spouse's
Drawbacks	● Rarely adjusted for inflation, ultimately limiting your buying power ● Taxed at regular income tax rate ● Usually can't postpone start to reduce taxes ● May provide limited income

FIXED INCOME

HESITATE...AND LOSE

Did you ever wonder why up to 70% of US citizens die without a will, allowing state law to dictate what happens to their assets? Maybe it's because dying doesn't have a fixed date. So it's easy to put off until tomorrow or the next day the admittedly unpleasant prospect of your own death.

But you can't take that approach with your 401(k) withdrawals. You'll turn 70½

TACTICAL DECISIONS

You don't want to be forced to make decisions that affect your 401(k) in a hurry, since you can't change your mind once you start taking minimum required distributions at 70½. The smarter approach is to start thinking about your choices well before you turn 59½ and can withdraw without penalty. And if you're considering retiring at 55, start even sooner.

- Find out from your plan administrator what your distribution choices will be, since not all plans offer all the possible alternatives

- Consider the advantages of naming a specific person or people as beneficiary as a way to influence the amount you must take each year

- Compare the pros and cons of the different ways you can calculate life expectancy

- Figure the date you'll want to start receiving income and find out how much advance notice your plan administrator needs to meet that deadline

- Estimate the value of your estate, including the present value of your 401(k) to anticipate whether you should withdraw more than the minimum to reduce the amount that may be subject to estate taxes

...as advantages and some limitations.

SOCIAL SECURITY	401(k)
• Payments may begin between 62 and 70 at your discretion • Paid regularly every month • Adjusted for inflation, increasing your buying power • Lasts for your lifetime and your spouse's	• Amount of income limited only by returns on your investments • You choose investments • May roll some or all over to IRA • May take a lump-sum withdrawal • May be able to begin taking income at 59½ or postpone until 70½

• May provide a limited percentage of your retirement needs
• Percentage of benefit may be subject to income tax, based on total income
	• No guarantee that income will last for your lifetime or yours and your spouse's
	• After 70½, must take minimum required distributions
	  • Taxed at regular income tax rate
	  • Vulnerable to potential estate tax as well as income tax

MORE FLEXIBLE INCOME

on a specific day. By the following April 1, you not only need a specific strategy for taking money out of your 401(k). You have to act on it.

If you don't have a plan, or don't respond to your plan administrator's request to choose a withdrawal method, one of two things will happen. Your plan administrator will send you a check for either the amount the administrator calculates you must withdraw for the first year or for the total value of your account minus 20% withholding. Or you'll miss the deadline and owe a 50% penalty on the amount you should have withdrawn but didn't.

Either way, it costs you. The penalty is an obvious financial loss, and the minimum distribution may be as well. That's because whatever method of calculating the minimum required distribution your administrator has used is the one you must use for all future distributions.

Taking Your Lump Sums

Many plans offer a lump-sum distribution.

With some 401(k) plans, you may have only two choices: rolling over the value of your account to an IRA or taking a lump-sum distribution in cash.

To cash or not to cash your 401(k): That is the question.

Your initial reaction to taking a lump sum may be that having the money in your own hands is the most, not the least, appealing option. You don't have to worry about setting up a withdrawal schedule or naming a beneficiary. You don't owe any management fees to the plan provider. And you can do anything you choose with the money.

But there's another side to the story. By taking a lump-sum distribution, you're giving up the benefit of tax deferral. That has short-term as well as long-term consequences. If you invest the lump sum to produce interest or dividends, they're taxable in the year you receive them. So are any capital gains. As a consequence, at least 15% and probably more of your investment earnings go straight to Uncle Sam. Over the long term, the effect of taking money from your earnings to pay taxes results in a dramatic reduction of earning potential.

But the most immediate drawback may be that you owe income tax on the full amount of the distribution. That amount could easily be large enough to bump your adjusted gross income for the year into the highest federal tax bracket. And you'll owe state income tax as well unless you live in one of the few states that doesn't impose one.

FORWARD AVERAGING

The only way to limit the tax you owe on a lump-sum distribution is to have been born before 1936—something you can't do much about now. But if you were, you may be able to use ten-year **forward averaging** and/or the capital gains election.

With forward averaging, you figure the tax you owe on your distribution as if you received it in equal installments over ten years rather than all at once, although you have to pay the full tax bill for the year in which you took the distribution. For example, instead of figuring tax on

one lump sum of $250,000, you'd divide that total by 10, figure the tax on $25,000 and then multiply that amount by ten.

The catch is that you must use 1986 tax rates, when the top rate was 50% rather than the current maximum of 39.6%. Even so, the tax you owe is likely to be less than if you figured it in the usual way if your 401(k) account has a

Form **4972**

Department of the Treasury
Internal Revenue Service
Name of recipient of distribu

Part I   Complete

1   Was this a distribut
    kind (pension, profit
2   Did you roll over a
3   Was this distribution
    who had been born be
4   Were you a plan part
    plan for at least 5 years
    If you answered "No" co
5a Did you use Form 4972 af
    form for a 1999 distributio
 b If you are receiving a
    for a previous

THE STOCK EXCEPTION

There is one time when taking a lump-sum distribution may pay dividends—sometimes big ones. If your employer has contributed company stock to your plan and it has increased in value, you may be able to take the stock as a lump-sum withdrawal. You pay the income tax at your regular rate on your **basis**, which is the value of the stock at the time it went into your account. You can postpone tax on your net unrealized appreciation (NUA) until you sell the stock at some point in the future. Those gains are then taxed at the capital gains rate, which is lower than your regular rate.

If you're doing forward averaging of a distribution that includes company stock, the calculations can be more complex than if you take just the stock as a distribution. You'll probably want to get some professional tax advice in that case.

PRESERVING CHOICE

Taking a lump-sum distribution isn't an all-or-nothing deal (unless you plan to use forward averaging).

One solution, if you need some cash, is to take some but not all of your assets as a lump sum. You'll owe the tax that's due. But if having the money lets you make a major investment, buy a new home, or pay for something that's important to you, the decision may be a wise one.

In a different circumstance,

COMPANY STOCK

LUMP SUM

if your spouse is the beneficiary of your 401(k) and you die before he or she turns 59½, there may be a tax advantage to taking a partial lump-sum distribution from your 401(k) before rolling the balance into an IRA. That's because, according to tax law, the money in your 401(k) account is **income in respect of a decedent,** or available to your spouse as the direct result of your death. When that's the case, the 10% early withdrawal penalty does not apply.

But once your spouse rolls over the money into an IRA, a withdrawal before he or she turns 59½ could be subject to the 10% penalty despite the fact that the money actually came from the same source, your 401(k). Of course, if your spouse has other sources of cash, preserving the tax-deferred status of your 401(k) account is probably wiser than taking a distribution.

If you're wondering why this strategy applies only to your spouse, it's because no other beneficiary has the right to roll over your 401(k) into an IRA in his or her own name. So there's no reason to make a withdrawal in anticipation of possibly needing the cash.

value of $250,000 or less. Smaller totals generally yield greater savings.

You report forward averaging on IRS Form 4972, which walks you through the steps you must follow to figure what you owe.

ELIGIBILITY RULES

To qualify for forward averaging you must:

- Have been born before 1936
- Take the entire amount of your 401(k) as a lump-sum distribution in a single tax year
- Have participated in your 401(k) for at least five years
- Not have used forward averaging for a distribution since 1986

No Place Like the Office

You may be able to leave your 401(k) account in your employer's plan when you retire.

Your employer may give you the option of leaving your 401(k) assets in the company plan after you retire.

There are some advantages, provided you're happy with the investment choices the plan provides. Staying put preserves your account's tax-deferred status and the option of rolling your account into an IRA at some point in the future. You don't have to find a new custodian for your account or look for new investments. And since the plan administrator is responsible for handling minimum distribution requirements after you turn 70½, that could make your life a lot simpler.

There may be some drawbacks, too, which might be serious enough to make you reject the option of leaving your money where it is. You may pay management fees that are higher than you'd pay with an IRA. Further, the plan may require you to begin taking money out as soon as you retire rather than being able to postpone withdrawals until

they're mandatory after 70½. But if the plan is your primary source of retirement income, and if you're reluctant to take responsibility for meeting distributions requirements, it may be the most appealing solution.

WHAT A DIFFERENCE A FEE MAKES

If the difference between paying 1% and 2% of your 401(k) assets as investment fees seems too small to worry about, consider this:

If you invest $60,000 over 30 years and earn an average return of 10% on your investments after the fees you owe are subtracted, you'll have a portfolio worth $345,437 before taxes. But if you pay just one percentage point more in fees, reducing your average return to 9%, you'll accumulate just $286,246. And if your fees reduce your return to 8%, your total will be $237,895. That's a $107,542 hit.

HANDLING WITHDRAWALS

When you're ready to begin taking distributions, either when you retire or at any time until you reach 70½, when you can't postpone any longer, you'll have to make a series of choices. Your plan administrator will give you a written description of those alternatives and will require a decision within 30 to 90 days. You may be able to make your choice as soon as seven days after getting the information, but if you wait longer than 90, the process must start again.

In relatively rare instances, you may be offered the option of liquidating your assets to buy a qualified **immediate annuity**, sometimes called a life annuity or an income annuity. The annuity pays you income on a regular schedule, usually guaranteed to last your lifetime, or the joint lifetime of you and your beneficiary.

In some plans, you may be able to take your distributions from your existing investment portfolio. In that case, your plan provider pays your distribution on a regular schedule by liquidating some of your assets each time, either on a percentage basis from each of your investments or according to instructions you provide.

You may also be able to take installment withdrawals over a fixed period of

PENSION MAX

Pension maximization, sometimes shortened to **pension max**, is a scheme to increase your current income while providing for a surviving spouse. What you do is elect a single life annuity (which provides larger payments than a joint and survivor annuity) and then use a portion of your income to pay the premiums on a life insurance policy in your name.

The theory is that when you die, and your annuity payments end, the insurance benefit will meet your spouse's income needs. There are drawbacks to this strategy, though, including the cost of the insurance itself, the commission you pay to the person who sells you the policy, and the responsibility it puts on your spouse for investing the death benefit to provide adequate income.

time or receive a specific dollar amount each year. Those choices may give you more flexibility than many annuities because you may be able to take a lump-sum withdrawal at any time without penalty. That's known as a **commutable** arrangement.

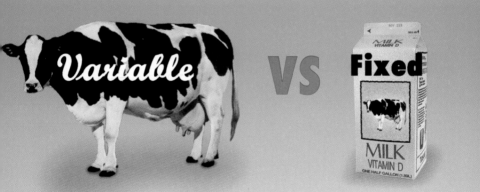

If you convert your assets to an immediate annuity, you may also have a choice between a **variable income annuity** and a **fixed income annuity**.

With a variable annuity, you select the way your assets are distributed among the fund alternatives the annuity offers, much as you allocate your contributions among the investment alternatives your 401(k) offers. The amount of income you receive with each payment depends on the actual return provided by annuity funds you have chosen and the **assumed interest rate (AIR)** you select. Generally speaking, your income increases in periods

when the return on the annuity funds you've selected increases, and dips if their return falters.

With a fixed annuity, the insurance company is responsible for paying income at the rate the contract specifies. You don't have to make any decisions, and you can expect to receive the same income over a fixed period of time. The advantage is that you'll always have a steady source of income. But the drawbacks are that you are likely to lose buying power as the cost of living increases, and you usually can't change the distribution schedule.

Payout Options

You may be able to choose the way your income is paid.

If you convert your 401(k) assets to a guaranteed stream of income, you may be able to choose the way the income is paid. If you're married, though, you'll probably have to select a joint and survivor payout unless your spouse agrees in writing to a different method.

One advantage of this approach is that the payments are calculated to meet your annual minimum distribution requirement.

WHAT WORKS FOR YOU?

While some payment plans offer more income options than others, or use different language to describe the alternatives they offer, you generally have a number of choices with different characteristics. That means you can choose the one that will work best for you.

PAYOUT OPTION	How payout amount is determined
SINGLE LIFE	Based on value of 401(k) assets, your age when payments begin, and interest rate (if fixed income) or investment performance and AIR (if variable income)
LIFE INCOME WITH PERIOD, OR TERM, CERTAIN	Based on value of 401(k) assets, your age when payments begin, interest rate (if fixed income) or investment performance and AIR (if variable income), and the length of the term (typically 5 to 20 years)
LIFE INCOME WITH REFUND PAYOUT	Based on value of 401(k) assets, your age when payments begin, interest rate (if fixed income) or investment performance and AIR (if variable income), and the refund guarantee
JOINT AND SURVIVOR LIFE	Based on value of 401(k) assets, your age and the age of your joint annuitant when payments begin, and interest rate (if fixed income) or investment experience and AIR (if variable income)
JOINT AND SURVIVOR PAYOUT WITH PERIOD CERTAIN	Based on value of 401(k) assets, your age and the age of your joint annuitant when payments begin, interest rate (if fixed income) or investment performance and AIR (if variable income), and the length of the term (typically 5 to 20 years)
FIXED AMOUNT (AVAILABLE ONLY WITH A FIXED INCOME PAYOUT)	You say how much income you want
FIXED PERIOD	Payment amount is determined by the length of time you choose to receive income, the value of 401(k) assets, interest rate (if fixed income) or investment performance and AIR (if variable income)

BENCHMARK RATES

If you choose a variable annuity you must choose an **assumed interest rate (AIR)** also known as your benchmark or hurdle rate. That's because the rate—usually in a range between 3% and 6%—becomes the standard against which annuity fund performance is measured. If your portfolio returns beat the benchmark, your annuity income goes up. If the returns are lower, your income drops.

For example, if your AIR is 3% and your average return is 5%, your income for the period will increase. But if your AIR is 6% and your return is 5%, your income will drop.

The AIR you choose is multiplied against your account value to determine the amount of your initial income payment. While choosing the lower rate initially provides a smaller income, setting a lower hurdle creates the potential for greater increases over time.

How long payout lasts	Pros	Cons
Income lasts for your lifetime	• Income as long as you live • The highest amount of income available in a lifetime payment plan	• When you die the payments stop, even if that occurs shortly after your payout begins, which means heirs may not get back the full value of your contract
Income lasts for your lifetime or at least as long as the term you select if you die sooner	• Income as long as you live • Beneficiary continues to get income for remaining term certain if you die before it expires	• Income amount will be less than with single life annuity
Income lasts for your lifetime or until all of the refundable value of the contract has been paid to your beneficiary after your death	• Income as long as you live • Your beneficiary continues to get income if you die before the contract value has been paid out	• Income amount will be less than with life annuity and probably than life with period certain (depending on length of the period certain)
Income lasts for your lifetime and the lifetime of your joint annuitant	• Income as long as you and your joint annuitant live • Flexibility in setting amount of second annuitant's income	• Each payment less than with single life alternatives (though can last longer) • No payment to beneficiary upon death of both annuitants
Income lasts for your lifetime and your joint annuitant's lifetime, or at least as long as the term selected if you both die sooner	• Income as long as you and your joint annuitant live • Beneficiary continues to get income for remaining term certain if you and your joint annuitant die	• Income amount will be less than with joint and survivor annuity without period certain
The time the payments will last is based on the contract value and interest rate at the time payments begin	• Potentially the highest amount of income (but the larger the payment the shorter the time frame) • Commutable	• No lifetime guarantee, so you may outlive your income, since all of your assets will be gone at the end of the term
You choose how long you want payments to last	• You know how long income will be coming in • Commutable	• No lifetime guarantee, so you may outlive your income, since all of your assets will be gone at the end of the term

Just Roll It Along

You don't have to move mountains to roll over your 401(k).

When you retire, you can move some or all of your 401(k) assets into an **individual retirement account** or **individual retirement annuity**—both referred to as **IRAs**. In fact, if you wish, you can divide the total value of your 401(k) among a number of IRAs if you want to name different beneficiaries for portions of your total retirement savings account.

There are lots of good reasons to choose an IRA. Being able to select your own investments is at the top of the list, along with the ability to control the amount you pay in fees and to determine which assets to liquidate to meet your minimum distribution requirements.

Among the drawbacks that you may want to consider before making this choice are that you can't borrow from an IRA as you sometimes can from your 401(k), and you can't postpone required withdrawals after you turn 70½, even if you're still working.

IRA: ACCOUNT OR ANNUITY?

An individual retirement account and an individual retirement annuity are alike in several important ways: They both provide the advantage of tax-deferred earnings, and they both require minimum distributions based on life expectancy and the value of your account. In both cases, the amounts you withdraw are taxed at your regular income tax rates.

But there are also some differences, especially after your distributions begin. An **annuity**, which you buy from an insurance company, provides a regular stream of income, typically for as long as you, or you and your beneficiary, live, or for a specific period of time called a term certain or a period certain.

The amount you receive is calculated by the annuity company, based on a number of variables:

● The value of your account at the time distributions begin
● Your life expectancy or the term certain
● Whether you choose a fixed or variable rate of return
● The number of special features you add

If you choose a lifetime payout, the amount the annuity company distributes to you each year will be enough to meet the minimum distribution requirement.

With an **account**, you usually have a wider choice of investments than with a variable annuity. You generally have a more active role in determining how much you must withdraw, and are responsible for actually taking the money. Some custodians, however, offer a plan for converting your investments to cash distributions on a regular schedule.

In most cases, you pay more in fees for an annuity than for an account, reflecting the higher level of management costs. You are also often locked into the distribution schedule. That limits your flexibility to take larger withdrawals if you need them, or makes it expensive to do so.

ANNUITY ISSUES

You can roll over your 401(k) to an individual retirement annuity, and **annuitize**, or receive an annual income for life. Your annuity provider will calculate the amount you need to receive each year to cover your minimum required distribution.

Like an income annuity, an individual retirement annuity may limit your withdrawals to the payment that's determined at the time you purchase the contract. And you may pay separate fees to cover mortality and expense (M&E) charges.

Experts disagree about whether choosing an individual retirement annuity is a smart choice when you're rolling over your 401(k). Advocates say this type of IRA is the only one that guarantees income for life. Opponents argue that the added costs of owning an annuity can actually erode your retirement income and that the frequent lack of flexibility for making unscheduled withdrawals can hamper your financial decisionmaking.

WHERE THE MONEY GOES

You don't have to look very far to find a financial institution to act as custodian or trustee for your rollover IRA. Any place that offers regular IRAs also offers rollover IRAs. In all likelihood, that includes the bank or credit union where you do your checking, the brokerage firms where you have accounts, and companies that sell mutual funds or annuities.

Chances are your 401(k) plan provider would like to hold onto your business. Other institutions would like to get it. So it's a buyer's market. Here's a list of some of the things you may want to consider in making your choice:

- What range of investment choices or annuity funds will you have?
- Is there a financial adviser available if you or your beneficiary have questions or are looking for guidance?
- Is there a system in place to help you manage your required distributions if you want to use it?
- Is the custodian willing to accept your designation of beneficiary form if the standard one doesn't let you make the arrangements you want?
- Will you be able to take more than your required minimum distribution once you begin to take income from your rollover IRA?

IT'S A VEHICLE? IT'S A SHELL?

An IRA isn't actually an investment. It's an arrangement that allows you to deposit money with a custodian and tell the custodian where to invest it. You own the investments the custodian makes for you, but they're distinct from investments you own in your taxable accounts because they're held in the IRA.

That's why you might hear IRAs described as vehicles, shells, or umbrellas. Those terms are attempts to explain in visual shorthand something that's a mechanism for investing rather than the investment itself.

401(k) or Rollover IRA?

Though they're alike in some important ways, these plans aren't identical twins.

If you want to preserve the tax-deferred earning potential of your 401(k), you can either leave the money in your employer's plan or move it to an individual retirement account (IRA) when you retire.

In some ways, 401(k)s and rollover IRAs are very similar. With either, for example, you must eventually take annual distributions and pay tax on that income. And with either you can influence the amount you must take each year through the beneficiary you name.

But there are also important differences between the two. For instance, if you transfer your assets to an IRA, you generally have more control over how the money is invested than you do with a 401(k). But with that flexibility, you also have more responsibility for meeting your earnings targets and making withdrawal decisions.

PRESERVATION NEWS

When you move your assets from your 401(k) to your rollover IRA, it's considered a **cash transaction**, even if it's handled as an electronic transfer. All the assets you're moving—you don't have to

Rollover IRA

	CUSTODIANS	If you move your assets to an individual retirement account, you can choose any custodian you wish.
	INVESTMENT CHOICES	There are few limits on investment choices in an IRA, and you can divide your 401(k) assets among two or more IRAs and invest each differently if you wish.
	BENEFICIARY	You can name any beneficiary you choose, though you may need your spouse's written permission to roll over your 401(k) into an IRA if the 401(k) plan requires your spouse to be your beneficiary.
	DISTRIBUTION AMOUNT	You figure out how much you must take each year as your required distribution and which assets to liquidate so you'll have that amount of cash available.
MRA	**MINIMUM REQUIREMENT DISTRIBUTION**	You may take more than the required minimum distribution if you wish.
Accounts 1 2 3 4 or or	**RECEIVE PAYMENT**	You must figure the minimum required distribution for each of your IRAs separately. But you may total the amount to be withdrawn and take it all from one account, or from two or more accounts in any proportion you want.
NO LOAN	**LOAN**	You can't borrow from your IRA

move them all—are **liquidated**, or sold for their current cash value. That total goes to your new account, where it's immediately allocated to specific investments or annuity funds you've chosen or to a money market or other holding account until you decide. For example, if the value of your 401(k) account is $500,000, that's what goes into the IRA.

Of course, there's no way to predict what your account value will be at the time it's liquidated. It could be at its all-time high or it could be in the dumps. Once you initiate the transfer process, you probably can't interrupt it to prevent selling during a market drop. But if you choose your IRA investments wisely, you'll be as well positioned to take advantage of the next market rebound as you would if you'd left your money in the 401(k).

Ordinarily, you might be concerned about the tax consequences of liquidating investments that have increased in value. But with an IRA rollover, no tax is due if the transaction is a direct transfer or if you complete an indirect rollover within the 60-day period that's permitted by law.

THE CLOCK IS RUNNING
Retiring may seem easy. But it can be an amazingly intricate process, at least in part because you have to make some decisions you won't be able to change. To avoid being rushed, it's a good idea to get a head start. Three to five years before you plan to leave your job isn't too soon to start asking questions about health insurance, pension and Social Security income, and distribution choices for your 401(k).

401(k)

If you leave your assets in your 401(k), you do not choose the plan provider or plan administrator. Your employer does.	**PLAN ADMINISTRATOR**	
You must choose among the investments offered through the plan unless it offers a brokerage window. Some plans limit changes to your portfolio after you retire.	**INVESTMENT CHOICES**	PLAN
In many plans you must name your spouse as beneficiary and get his or her written permission to change your beneficiary or take more than your minimum required distribution.	**BENEFICIARY**	
You may use your plan assets to buy an income annuity, which pays the required annual minimum or set up withdrawals from plan.	**DISTRIBUTION AMOUNT**	ANNUITY
You may not be able to withdraw more than the annual minimum from a 401(k).	**MINIMUM REQUIRED DISTRIBUTION**	MRA
If you are responsible for figuring your minimum required distribution, you must calculate the amount separately for each 401(k) you have and take the correct amount from each account.	**RECEIVE PAYMENT**	Accounts 1 2 3 4
You may be able to borrow from your 401(k) even after you retire.	**LOAN**	LOAN POSSIBLE

A Time to Retire

There are almost as many retirement timetables as there are people retiring.

The idea that you retire at 65 may be common knowledge, but it's no longer common practice. In fact, 40% of US workers retire before they're 60, and another 27% by the time they're 64. At the same time, you probably know a number of people who work full-time well into their 70s.

If you're still working out your own timetable for retirement, it pays to keep in mind the types of benefits you may be eligible for at different ages.

RETIREMENT LOCAL

AGE	ARRIVAL
55	EARLY RETIREMENT
59½	PENALTY FREE WITHDRAWALS
62	SOCIAL SECURITY (EARLY)
65	MEDICARE
70	SOCIAL SECURITY (LATE)
70½	REQUIRED WITHDRAWALS
75	LAST CALL FOR 403(b)S

If you retire anytime after you turn 55, you may begin withdrawing from your 401(k) plan without owing a federal 10% penalty on early withdrawals. Your employer may also begin paying your pension if you are eligible for one. However, you don't qualify for Medicare yet, so you must make your own health insurance arrangements if you are not covered through your former employer's plan.

You may begin taking money from your 401(k) without owing a 10% early withdrawal penalty, and you can take as much or as little as you choose. However, your employer's plan may not allow withdrawals if you're still working for the company.

AN EARLY (RETIREMENT) WARNING

Early retirement can put a strain on your long-term financial security. To begin with, if your surviving spouse will be dependent on your Social Security as a primary source of income, the reduced payment can be a serious handicap over the long term.

In addition, many defined benefit pensions reduce the amount you collect if you're younger than 65 when you retire. If that income is paid over 30 or 40 years, even a small annual reduction can add up to a lot of money. For example, a 15% reduction on an $18,000 pension would be $2,700 a year, or $81,000 over a 30-year retirement.

And keep in mind that when you stop earning income, you can't make additional contributions to your 401(k) or to an IRA. If you've been adding $5,000 a year to your account and retire five years early, you'll put $25,000 less set aside. That reduces the principal on which tax-deferred earnings may accumulate.

None of this means you shouldn't retire when you please. But a smaller income over potentially long periods is an important consideration as you make your plans.

If your spouse has died, you're eligible for retirement benefits from Social Security based on his or her contributions. If you're still working, or you'll qualify for benefits based on your own contributions, you should get in touch with the Social Security Administration (SSA) and your financial adviser to see which payment option works best for you.

 This is the earliest date you qualify to receive Social Security income based on your own contributions. If you were born before 1938, you'll get 80% of the benefit you'd qualify for at 65. If you were born after that date, you'll get less. And, if you work and earn more than the annual limit set by Congress, you'll lose some of your Social Security benefits.

 Though it's not always the official start of retirement, age 65 remains a key moment in several ways. It's the first time you're eligible for Medicare. If you were born before 1938, it's the age you can start getting your full Social Security retirement benefit. And, after you're 65, there's no cap on the amount you can earn and still continue to collect your full benefit.

Age 65 is likely to lose some of its cache as the retirement age, however, as the age for collecting full Social Security benefits creeps up to 66, and then 67.

 There's no point in further postponing Social Security income, since the annual bonuses you receive for delaying payment are capped at age 70. The base benefit you qualify for at this age is the most you'll get.

 For the year you turn 70½, you must make your first required withdrawal from your 401(k), any traditional IRAs (including rollover IRAs), and any annuities you have purchased with tax-deferred income. The only exception—for 401(k)s but not IRAs or annuities—is if you're still working.

After 70½, you can't make any additional contributions to a traditional IRA, though you can put earned income into a Roth IRA if you qualify, based on your adjusted gross income.

 If you contributed to a 403(b) before 1986, you may be able to postpone withdrawals of those amounts until you're 75. Check with your plan administrator and your financial adviser.

IS SOONER BETTER?

Should you start to get income from Social Security at 62? The answer is usually yes—provided you're retired—because for 12 years or longer you'll be ahead of the game. For example, if your full annual benefit was $17,196, you'd get $13,757 at 62. When you reached 74, you would have collected $165,084 (before increases for inflation). But if you'd waited until you were 65 to collect, at age 74, you would have received $154,764. But from that age on, having waited pays off.

Should you wait until you're 70 to start collecting? In most cases, especially be-

cause the limit on penalty-free earnings for people over 65 has been eliminated, the answer is no. If you qualified for $17,196 a year at 65, you'd get $23,016 if you waited until 70. But at age 84, you would have collected $326,724 (before increases for inflation) if you'd begun at 65 and $322,224 if you'd waited until 70.

The amount of time you come out ahead will be reduced slightly each year from now on, as the percentage of your full benefit you're eligible to collect at 62 slowly drops. But that doesn't alter the picture radically.

Withdrawals Have Their Limits

Rules tell you how much you must take from a 401(k), but not how much you can, or should, take.

The federal government is explicit about how much you must take from your 401(k) each year after you turn 70½. The amount is based on:

- Your official life expectancy, or the joint life expectancy of you and your beneficiary
- The value of your account, revised annually

The same requirements apply to retirement savings in a traditional IRA, including any you open with money you roll over or transfer from your 401(k). The rules also apply to income annuities purchased with 401(k) assets, and cover a whole range of other retirement savings plans, including plans at a former job, contributions you made for self-employment, or income you received from a partnership.

But nobody tells you what you should take each year to have enough money to live the way you want while making sure that your assets will last as long as you do.

KEEPING IT UP

The rate of return you achieve on your 401(k) assets while you're contributing is a key factor in determining the long-term value of your account. It's no surprise that an average annual return of 10% produces a substantially larger account value than a return of 6%. But as retirement years stretch out, it's equally important to achieve a strong return on the money in your account.

That's one of the reasons many retirement advisers stress the importance of holding equities—including stocks and stock mutual funds—in your 401(k) account much later into retirement than has traditionally been recommended. In the past, advisers often suggested that you allocate a percentage of your portfolio equal to your age to fixed-income investments. In other words, if you

were 65, then 65% of your holdings would be in bonds and similar investments. But you're increasingly apt to hear that, at 65, up to 65% of your tax-deferred portfolio should still be in equities.

The shift to higher equity allocation is to allow you, when you begin withdrawing, to take as much as you're required to take, and perhaps more, without running out of money. The risk, of course, is that the equity markets can drop at any time, reducing the value of your account and the amount that you can afford to withdraw without reducing your principal.

MAKING A PLAN
There's no one right way to rake in retirement

A → Bonds → Money you can spend

B | C → Hold for 10 years → Equities / Stocks / Don't Touch

ANTICIPATING THE INEVITABLE

While your minimum required distribution is based on life expectancy rather than stated as a percentage, what you withdraw is a percentage of your account value. For example, anyone who begins withdrawals with a life expectancy of 19.4 will have to take out 5.15% of his or her account value.

A HYPOTHETICAL PLAN

There's no way to protect yourself completely from volatility in the equity markets without risking slow death by inflation. But there may be ways to produce a stream of income while maintaining some long-term growth.

One possible approach, which you might consider if you've moved your 401(k) assets to an IRA, or if your 401(k) is in a brokerage account, is to think about your retirement as a series of three ten-year periods. To provide the income you need for each of those periods, divide your total account into thirds.

Invest one-third in secure fixed-income investments, such as an annuity with a ten-year fixed term payout period or a series of bonds with staggered maturity dates—a **ladder**—designed so that one

income, but you need some plan.

bond matures each year for ten years. Spend the income these investments produce. If you've created a bond ladder, you may need to withdraw some or all of the principal of the maturing bond to meet your minimum distribution requirement.

Invest the remaining two-thirds in equities and don't withdraw that principal or the earnings it produces for ten years. If the market is strong for much of the period, and you manage your investments wisely, they have potential to grow significantly in value. And even if there are periods of slow growth or market declines, not having to liquidate those assets may give your portfolio enough time to recover and resume growth.

Then, when the first ten-year period ends, begin the cycle again.

Here's a hypothetical example of this approach:

Suppose the value of your account when you begin is $300,000. You invest $100,000 in $10,000 bonds, one maturing each year for ten years, and the remaining $200,000 in equities, seeking an annualized return of 10% annually for ten years.

When the first third of your account is gone, your remaining assets may be worth as much as $518,748 before taxes. Then you can follow the same approach once more, allocating a third of your assets to spending, and investing the rest.

But remember, there are no guarantees in investing. It's smart to work with a financial adviser before you invest. And you must weigh the risks of losing money against potential returns.

at 10%

A **B** **C**

Bonds

Equities **Stocks** **Hold for 10 years**

Don't Touch

Money you can spend

To reduce the percentage you must withdraw, and extend the life of your account, you have to lengthen your life expectancy by naming a beneficiary. For example, if instead of 19.4, you begin with a life expectancy of 26.1, you must take only 3.83% of your account balance.

Each year, as your life expectancy decreases, the percentage of your account

that you're required to withdraw increases. If the account is not growing at least as fast as you're taking money out, it will eventually run dry. That's okay, provided neither you nor anyone else needs the income. In fact, that's the government's idea of how retirement savings plans should work.

Managing Withdrawals

Somewhere between a withdrawal that's too large and one that's too small is one that's just right.

Before you start making required withdrawals from your 401(k) or IRA rollover, you need a plan for how much to take and when to take it, to be sure that you are:
- Withdrawing the required minimum
- Providing enough income to meet your financial needs
- Continuing to take advantage of tax-deferred growth

DIFFERENT PATHS TO CASH

If you buy an income annuity with your 401(k) assets, or roll those assets into an individual retirement annuity, you establish a payment schedule with the annuity provider at the time of purchase. While the responsibility for taking the correct amount is legally yours, the annuity provider guarantees that the amount you get will satisfy the federal requirement for minimal distributions and that you will receive income for life.

If you move your assets to a traditional IRA, you have more responsibility for making sure you take at least the required minimum each year. In many cases, you can set up a regular distribution schedule with your custodian that will meet the required minimum. But some custodians' plans give you more control than others over which assets to liquidate, or allow you more flexibility to change the amount you withdraw if your financial needs change.

HOT DATES

You have until December 31 to take your required minimum distribution from your retirement savings for the year. But if you're setting your own schedule, you can take the money as early as January if you prefer, in equal installments during the year, or whenever you need some cash.

You can figure out how much you have to take as a minimum distribution as soon as your account is valued for the previous year. That means, for example, the amount of your minimum 2002 distribution is determined by the value of your account on December 31, 2001, divided by your official life expectancy.

Three Ways

Lump sum?

You can take a lump sum.
Once you calculate the amount you must withdraw for the year, you can take it at any time by liquidating assets in your 401(k) or IRA rollover and moving the money to your regular checking or savings account.

For example, if your equity investments increase dramatically in value in a stock market rally, you might decide to sell enough shares to equal the amount you must take for the year. While there's no way to time the market so that you always sell at the very top, the only way you can be forced to sell at the bottom is if you wait until the last few days of the year and prices drop.

On the other hand, one advantage of waiting until the end of the year is that you can pick up an additional 12 months of tax-deferred earnings. If your investment returns are strong during the year, your account value can get a big boost.

A COMMON MISTAKE

One mistake it's easy to make is to assume that if you have mutual fund distributions paid to you rather than reinvested in your account, you'll be taking the right amounts. It might happen—by coincidence. But most of the time you'll be off the mark one way or the other.

If the return you're getting on your retirement savings averages 10% in a year you're obligated to take only 6.25%—for example, at age 70½, when your single life expectancy is 16—you can take it all without penalty. But if your return is averaging 5% in a year you're required to take 8%—when your official single life expectancy is 12.5 years, at age 75—you'll be faced with a 50% penalty on the amount you don't take.

Further, since the return you'll get on your investments isn't predictable, it's hard to plan your living expenses or be sure you'll be able to pay your bills if you're just taking distributions as they come.

to Withdraw

You can take income as you need it.
If you've got other regular sources of income, you can withdraw from your retirement savings account when you need extra cash—to pay quarterly bills such as insurance or estimated taxes, for example, to make gifts, take trips, or meet extra ordinary medical expenses.

The potential drawbacks of this approach are not taking enough to satisfy the minimum requirement or dipping too far into your principal too soon, which could put your future financial security at risk.

You can set up a regular schedule.
If your retirement savings income is an essential part of your living expenses, you may find it easier to manage your cash flow by taking a regular amount on a regular schedule, as if you were earning a salary. One appeal of regular withdrawals is that you don't risk forgetting to withdraw, or have to liquidate your assets in a rush to meet the minimal withdrawal for the year.

You can work with your financial adviser to set up a long-term liquidation plan. Or you can work actively with the adviser to decide which assets to liquidate at a particular time.

If you're selling off equity assets each month to provide income, you may have to sell more shares in some months and fewer in others—a kind of dollar cost averaging in reverse. For example, if your stock mutual fund's net asset value (NAV) is $25, you'd have to sell 100 shares to produce $2,500 in income. If the NAV rises to $30, you'd have to sell just 83⅓ shares, and if it drops to $20, you'd have to sell 125 shares.

> **TAX TIP**
> Where you live may affect the income tax you owe. That's because some states don't tax retirement account distributions. And a state can tax you and your assets only if it's your permanent residence. That's usually determined by factors such as where you vote, where you register your cars, and where you own real estate.

Taxing Issues

You can play the tax game to your advantage
if you make the right moves.

If you find yourself in the enviable position
of having several sources of retirement
income, what do you spend first?

Most retirement advisers agree: Don't
touch your 401(k) or other tax-deferred
investments before you turn 70½, unless
it's your only source of income. Start
taking your pension if you can't postpone
it, begin collecting Social Security, and
draw on your taxable investments before
touching your 401(k).

The reason for this strategy: Taxes.

ECONOMIC LOGIC

The longer your tax-deferred assets are
left undisturbed and can produce earnings, the more potential they have to
increase in value, perhaps substantially.
For example, $200,000 returning 10% a
year can grow to $518,748 in ten years. If
your life expectancy was 20 years, that
would mean you could take a minimum
distribution of almost $26,000 rather than
$10,000, a significant dif-
ference in dollars and in
your sense of security.

In the case of your
taxable investments,
you're already paying
income tax on any
dividends or taxable interest
you earn. So you're usually better off withdrawing and spending this money rather
than incurring additional tax on amounts
you withdraw from tax-deferred accounts.
What's more, if you begin
withdrawing from
your tax-deferred
accounts, you can
also end up in a
higher tax bracket
and have to pay at a
higher rate on the
amounts you withdraw.

TAX TIP

Where you live may affect the income tax
you owe. That's because some states don't
tax retirement account distributions. And a
state can tax you and your assets only if it's
your permanent residence. That's usually
determined by factors such as where you
vote, where you register your cars, and
where you own real estate.

If you
sell off taxable
investments
you've held for
more than a year to
produce the income you
need, the tax you'll owe on
any increase in value will be
taxed at the lower capital gains
rate, rather than at your regular
income tax rate. That can be a difference
of almost 20 percentage points if you're in
the highest bracket. Those savings will
increase for investments you buy in 2000
or later and hold for at least five years.
Any gains you realize on that part of your
portfolio will be taxed at 18% (vs. 20%) if
you're in the 28% or higher bracket and at
8% (vs. 10%) if you're in the 15% bracket.

A STEP UP IN BASIS, DOWN IN TAX

No rule of thumb applies to everyone. If
you're in poor health, it might be wiser to
spend the money in your tax-deferred plan
and hold onto your taxable investments.
That's because if you leave taxable investments to your beneficiaries in your will,
these investments are **stepped up in
basis**. That means that their monetary
worth is determined on the date your
estate is valued.

If your beneficiary sells an asset that's
been stepped up in value, any gain is
based on the stepped-up value, not on
what you paid for the asset. For example,
if you bought 100 shares of stock at $50 a
share that was worth $75 a share when
your estate was valued, the stepped-up
value would be $7,500, not $5,000. So if
your beneficiary sold the stock at $80 a
share, the gain would be only $500
($8,000 – $7,500) rather than $3,000
($8,000 – $5,000).

The tax disadvantage of tax-deferred
investments is that they can't be transferred by will and they are not stepped up
in value. The beneficiary you name can't
sell the asset (though he or she could take

DIFFERENT BITES

Estate taxes are taxes imposed by the federal government and some state governments if the value of the assets you own when you die is more than the amount offset by the unified credit. Your estate pays those taxes, though your executor may have to sell assets that would otherwise go to your heirs in order to pay the bill.

Inheritance taxes are state taxes your heirs pay based on the value of the property they inherit from you. If you wish, you can include a provision in your will instructing your executor to pay these taxes from the estate as well, so that your heirs don't face the possibility of having to sell their inheritance to pay the amount that's due.

The two are often described together as death taxes.

a lump-sum withdrawal), and must pay income tax on all distributions.

But don't get the wrong idea. If your beneficiary is able to spread income from your retirement assets over an extended period, the benefits will far outweigh the tax liability.

THE OTHER TAX

While you're investigating the tax consequences of withdrawals from your retirement savings accounts, it's easy to lose sight of the possibility that your estate will owe federal taxes when you die. That tax is in addition to the income taxes your beneficiary will pay on the amounts he or she withdraws after the estate taxes are paid.

Not everyone has to worry about estate taxes. But the more you accumulate in retirement savings, the greater the risk you run. If the total value of your assets is $700,000 or more, you may need to take the potential tax consequences seriously, since the rates begin at 37% and quickly reach 55%. The assets that count in calculating the value of your estate include your:

MY ESTATE

- 401(k)
- Other tax-deferred plans
- Taxable investments
- Life insurance policy's face value
- Home and other real property
- Half of whatever you own jointly with another person

The $700,000 isn't an arbitrary number. The federal government limits the size of the estate you can leave tax free by giving each person a **unified gift and estate tax credit**. In 2001, that credit allows you to leave an estate worth $675,000 without getting hit with estate taxes. In 2003 and 2004, the amount is scheduled to increase to $700,000, eventually rising to $1,000,000 in 2006. (However, there is some pressure in Congress to eliminate estate taxes altogether.)

THE BETTER HALF

Half the value of anything you own jointly with your spouse belongs to your spouse. That amount isn't part of your estate. But if you own property jointly with anyone other than your spouse, its full value is included in the estate of the first owner to die.

Expert Guidance

You don't have to strike out into new 401(k) territory on your own.

You're likely to be more confident about naming beneficiaries and making withdrawal decisions if you've got an experienced guide to answer your questions and suggest routes to your goals. But having help is more than just comforting. Since many of the decisions you have to make are irrevocable, you don't want to risk making a mistake. So working with an experienced retirement planner can help you avoid the pitfalls.

FINDING HELP
Though the ideal adviser isn't likely to appear out of the blue, you may find the help you need close to home. Your employer may have one or more specialists on staff whose job is to provide information, if not retirement advice. That person will know the ins and outs of your plan, and how other employees have handled the issues you're facing.

The financial institutions where you have checking or investment accounts may also provide advisers. Keep two things in mind, though. Just because someone works for a bank, credit union, or brokerage firm doesn't mean that person has the experience necessary to serve as your adviser. You should always ask for professional credentials and a summary of retirement-planning experience before taking someone's advice. Second, you may prefer impartial advice from people who would have nothing to gain financially from the decisions you make.

EXTENDING A RELATIONSHIP
If you already have a good working relationship with one or more financial advisers, ask them whether they're qualified to work with you on retirement issues. If it's not their area of expertise, ask them to recommend a colleague or professional associate. Using advisers who are comfortable working together can make your life simpler, and help you put together the pieces of your retirement plan.

For example, rather than assuming you'll withdraw all of your 401(k) and IRA assets before you die, an adviser should take them into account in your estate plan. The larger your account balance, the more important it is that those retirement assets aren't overlooked since there could be substantial tax consequences for your beneficiaries.

THE SELECTION PROCESS
There's no single right way to choose an adviser, but there are some guidelines that can help.

Step 1

Decide on the qualifications you're seeking. Two of the most important are credentials and experience. Ask about an adviser's formal education, on-the-job training, and professional accreditation, as well as how long he or she has been providing retirement-planning advice. A minimum of five years' experience and a professional certification or license isn't too much to ask.

Don't forget compatibility, though. You have to be comfortable with your adviser as well as confident of his or her abilities. Otherwise, you're unlikely to ask for advice or take it when it's given.

JUST A CLICK AWAY
A number of financial institutions and 401(k) specialists have developed extensive retirement-planning websites, providing customized advice as well as do-it-yourself tools such as calculators and worksheets.

You might want to visit one or more of these sites in addition to working with a personal adviser. If nothing else, the experience can trigger questions—or solutions—you might not have thought of.

THE QUESTIONS TO ASK

Make a list of questions to ask an adviser and be sure to ask them. If you've written them down, you're less likely to get distracted and forget. At this point, what you really want to know is how responsive the adviser is and how direct the answers are.

Here are some of the key questions:

- Could you explain the pros and cons of rolling over a 401(k) into an IRA?
- What's your advice on reallocating my investment portfolio after retirement?
- What advice can you give about making retirement assets last as long as they're needed?
- What factors are most important in naming a beneficiary?
- Who are your typical clients?
- How are you paid for your services?

Step 4

Make your choice. You may know right away which adviser you prefer to work with, or you may have to weigh two finalists against each other. At that point, the range of services offered and the cost of the advice can be deciding factors.

Step 3

Conduct interviews. Call the people on your preliminary list, explaining that you are ready to make retirement decisions and are looking for an adviser. If a person is interested, and you are comfortable with the response, schedule an interview. Consider going to the adviser's office to get an impression of the tone and surroundings.

Before the interview begins, make a list of questions. Take a notebook with you and write down the answers as well as your overall impressions. That will make it easier to remember the interview later. And it might give you ideas about what to ask in your next interview.

Step 2

Get recommendations. Ask colleagues, friends, family, and your other professional advisers about retirement planners they've worked with. Go to seminars to watch potential advisers in action. Before you decide to work with anyone, ask for references and check them out.

SHOW AND TELL

Be prepared to answer some questions yourself as part of the interview process. To do an effective job, an adviser will need a sense of your overall financial situation, the estate planning you've done, and what your expectations are for the future.

Your adviser will also need a copy of your 401(k) plan document and your IRA agreement, not just copies of your beneficiary designations. Their terms have a direct impact on the decisions you can make and on what will happen to your assets if your wishes about beneficiaries and the way you plan to calculate life expectancy aren't officially on record.

Accumulation unit: Accumulation units are the shares you own in variable annuity subaccounts (also called investment portfolios or annuity funds) while you're putting money into an annuity. If your 401(k) plan includes an annuity, each time you make a pre-tax contribution, that amount is added to one or more subaccounts to buy additional accumulation units. The value of your account is figured by multiplying the number of units you own by the dollar value of each unit.

Account balance: Your account balance, also called your accrued benefit, is the amount your 401(k) account is worth on a date that it's valued. For example, if the value of your account on December 31 is $250,000, that's your account balance.

Your account balance is used to figure how much you must withdraw from your account each year, once you start taking required distributions. Specifically, your account balance at the end of your plan's fiscal year is divided by your life expectancy to determine the amount you must take from your account during the next fiscal year.

Annuitant: An annuitant is a person who receives income from an annuity. If you receive a distribution from an annuity that you or your employer buys with your 401(k) assets, you're the annuitant.

Similarly, you're the annuitant if you take distributions from an individual retirement annuity (IRA) or from an individual annuity you buy with after-tax income. If your beneficiary receives annuity income after your death, he or she becomes the annuitant.

Annuity unit: Annuity units are the shares you own in variable annuity subaccounts (also called investment portfolios or annuity funds) during the period you're receiving income from the annuity. The number of your annuity units is fixed at the time that you buy the income annuity contract, or when you annuitize your deferred variable annuity.

While the number of units does not change, the value of each unit fluctuates to reflect the performance of the underlying investments in the subaccount. That's why the income you receive from a variable annuity may differ from month to month.

Automatic enrollment: Your employer has the right to sign you up for your company's 401(k) plan, in what's known as an automatic, involuntary, or negative enrollment. If you don't want to participate, you must refuse, in writing, to be part of the plan.

In an automatic enrollment, the company determines the percentage of earnings you contribute and how your contribution is allocated. You have the right to change either or both of those choices if you stay in the plan. However, if you decide not to participate and take out the money that was put into your account, you'll owe the 10% early withdrawal penalty if you're younger than 59½.

Beneficiary: A beneficiary is the person or institution you designate to receive any assets left in your 401(k) account or IRA when you die. You may also name contingent beneficiaries who would be entitled to the assets if your primary beneficiary dies before you do, or chooses not to accept the assets. If you're married, you may be required to name your spouse as beneficiary of your 401(k), unless your spouse agrees in writing that you may make a different designation.

Blue sky laws: Blue sky laws require that investors get the information they need in order to make informed buy and sell decisions. These laws, passed by states rather than by the federal government, require companies offering stock, mutual funds, and other financial products to register them with the appropriate public agency and provide the financial details of each offering in writing.

Brokerage window: A 401(k) account that permits its plan participants to buy and sell investments through a designated brokerage account is said to offer a brokerage window. While the percentage of plans offering windows is increasing, opinion is divided on the wisdom of giving participants this wide a choice.

Cash balance plan: A cash balance plan is a defined benefit plan that has many of the characteristics of a defined contribution plan. The benefit you get is defined in terms of credits to a hypothetical account. Based on a percentage of current pay, the hypothetical account is credited with hypothetical earnings. These plans are portable, which makes them popular with younger and mobile workers. But they are often unpopular with older workers because their pensions may be less than with traditional defined benefit plan.

Cash value: Cash value is the amount that an account is worth at any given time. For example, the cash value of your 401(k) account is what your account is worth at the end of the plan year, often December 31.

The cash value of an insurance policy is the amount the insurer will pay you, based on your policy's cash reserve, if you cancel your policy. The cash value is the difference between the amount you paid in premiums and the actual cost of insurance plus other expenses.

Conduit IRA: A conduit IRA is an individual retirement account you establish with money you roll over from a 401(k) or other retirement savings plan. The purpose of a conduit IRA is to enable you to move your existing assets into a new employer's plan. You can also open a conduit IRA with money from a 403(b) plan, and roll it over into another 403(b). But you can't mix money from two different types of plans in one conduit IRA and roll the total into a new plan. Nor can you roll a conduit IRA into a new employer's plan if you've added money to the IRA from any other source.

Custodian: A custodian is an organization, such as a bank, brokerage firm, or mutual fund company, that's responsible for the assets of a 401(k) plan, mutual fund, or IRA. In other cases, a custodian may be a person who is responsible for making financial decisions on behalf of a minor child or disabled adult.

Death benefit: A death benefit is money your beneficiary collects from your 401(k) account or IRA if you die before you begin taking your minimum required distribution. In most cases, a beneficiary who receives a death benefit may take the full value of your account as a lump sum, or stretch out the income from your account over his or her life expectancy, a period that's determined by Internal Revenue Service actuarial tables.

Default provision: Default provisions are the terms and conditions of your 401(k) plan agreement or your IRA contract. They take effect if, when you

die, you haven't named a beneficiary, specified the way your life expectancy has been figured for your required distributions, or indicated the term over which your beneficiary should receive income. If your wishes about beneficiaries are in conflict with the default provisions of your plan or contract, you must be sure that your wishes are accepted and approved by the plan sponsor or IRA custodian before your death.

Defined benefit plan: A defined benefit plan provides a pension, or income, to retired employees. The amount you get usually depends on your age when you retire, your final salary, and the number of years you worked for your employer. The employer is responsible for funding the plan and investing its assets in order to have enough money to meet the company's pension obligations.

Defined contribution plan: A defined contribution plan is an employer sponsored retirement plan in which you and other participants have individual accounts. The retirement assets you accumulate are based on the amount that's contributed to your account, the investments that are chosen, and the earnings those investments produce after expenses. 401(k) plans are one type of defined contribution plan, as are profit sharing plans, 403(b) plans, 457 plans, and SIMPLE plans.

Distribution: A distribution is money paid from your 401(k) plan or IRA. You may take a distribution without penalty after you turn 59½, and in most cases you must begin taking distributions after you turn 70½. You may also take penalty-free distributions after age 55 if you retire early, or if you arrange to take a series of substantially equal payments from your account for a period of not less than five years, or until you turn 59½, whichever is longer.

In everyday usage, the terms distribution and withdrawal tend to be used interchangeably to mean money you take out of a 401(k) or IRA.

Excess accumulation: An excess accumulation is money you should have taken out of a 401(k) or IRA to meet your annual minimum required distribution but did not take. There is an annual 50% penalty on any excess accumulation, as well as income tax due on the amount when you do take it out of your account.

For example, if you have an excess accumulation of $10,000 for 2001, you owe $5,000 of it in penalty. If you still haven't taken the distribution by the end of 2002, you'll owe the remaining $5,000 in penalty.

Excess contribution: An excess contribution is aftertax money you put into your 401(k). You might choose to make an excess contribution if you have added the maximum pretax amount permitted by the federal government for the year, but have not reached the ceiling, stated as a percentage of salary, that your employer allows. For example, if the federal cap is $10,500 and your employer lets you contribute 15% of your salary, you'll reach the first limit before you reach the second one if you earn more than $70,000.

The advantage of making an excess contribution is that any earnings accumulate tax deferred. The disadvantages are that you can't roll over aftertax contributions into an IRA, and figuring the tax that's due on your required distributions may be complicated.

Expense ratio: The expense ratio is a percentage of the total value of your 401(k) account or IRA that you pay to a financial services company for management expenses. The higher your expense ratio, the less valuable the tax-deferred advantage of investing in a retirement savings plan becomes.

If your expense ratio, or the combined total of your expense ratio and your share of the plan's administrative expenses, is more than 3% of your account value, you may lose the advantage of tax-deferral entirely. Expense ratios for retail mutual funds are provided in the fund prospectus and published in the financial press.

Guaranteed investment contract (GIC): Your 401(k) plan may offer a guaranteed investment contract as one of its investment options. A GIC is a contract the plan sponsor negotiates with an insurance company to provide a fixed rate of return on your investment principal for a specific period of time. The insurance company assumes the investment risk of paying the guaranteed return. But there is usually a penalty, figured as a percentage of your account balance, if you want to move your money out of the GIC before the end of the term.

Hardship withdrawal: A hardship withdrawal occurs when you are allowed to take out some or all of your 401(k) money to meet certain financial needs. You qualify by meeting the conditions your plan imposes, which demonstrate the urgency of the situation and your need for the money. However, if you're younger than 59½, you must pay a 10% penalty plus income tax on the amount you withdraw, and you may not be able to contribute to the plan again for a year or more.

Highly compensated employees: Highly compensated employees are people who earned more than $85,000 in 2000 working for their employer. The percentage of earnings that highly compensated employees may contribute to their 401(k) plan is determined by the average percentage of earnings contributed by all lower-paid participants in the plan.

If lower-paid employees contribute an average 2% or less, higher-paid employees may contribute two times the percent. If the average is 3% to 8%, higher-paid employees may contribute two percentage points more. And if the average is 8% or higher, the maximum is 1.25 times the percent.

Income annuity: An income annuity, sometimes called an immediate annuity, pays an annual income, usually in monthly installments. The amount you receive is determined by the purchase price of the contract, your age (and the age of your beneficiary if you name one), the term over which the annuity will be paid, and the specific details of the contract.

You might buy an income annuity with assets from your 401(k) plan, or your plan may buy an income annuity on your behalf. The annuity provider guarantees an income that will satisfy your minimum required distribution.

Income in respect of a decedent: Any income your beneficiary receives after your death that would have gone to you if you were still alive is described as income in respect of a decedent. One example is the income your beneficiary gets as a minimum required distribution from your 401(k) or IRA. In this case, your beneficiary pays tax on that income at his or her ordinary rate, as you would have.

Inherited IRA: An inherited IRA is one that passes to a beneficiary at the death of the IRA owner. If you name your spouse as beneficiary of your IRA, your spouse inherits the IRA at your death. At that point, it is your spouse's property. But if you name anyone other than your spouse, that beneficiary inherits the rights to income from your IRA, which continues to be registered in your name, but not the IRA itself.

Insurance trust: You set up an insurance trust to own a life insurance policy on your life. When you die, the face value of the insurance policy is paid to the trust. That keeps the insurance payment out of your estate, while making money available to pay any estate tax that may be due.

If you're married, you may set up an insurance trust to buy a second-to-die policy, which pays face value at the death of the second spouse. That allows either you or your spouse to leave all assets to the other, postponing potential estate tax until the second one of you dies. At that point, the insurance benefit is available to pay any tax that might be due.

Life expectancy: Your life expectancy is the age to which you can expect to live. The IRS provides actuarial tables that establish your official life expectancy, which you use in calculating your minimum required distribution from a 401(k), traditional IRA, or other tax-deferred retirement savings plan. However, your true life expectancy, based on your lifestyle, family history, and other factors, may be longer or shorter than your official life expectancy.

Living payout rules: If you die after you begin taking your minimum required distribution from your 401(k) or traditional IRA, living payout rules determine how much money must be paid each year to your beneficiary. The living payout rules require that the assets in your account be paid out at least as quickly as they would have been paid had you continued to collect the income.

There are two exceptions, however. If your spouse is your beneficiary, your spouse may roll over your 401(k) account or IRA into a new account in his or her own name. Or, if your beneficiary isn't your spouse and is more than ten years younger than you, the minimum required distribution may be recalculated based on that person's actual life expectancy and yours, rather than dividing by a number determined by the minimum distribution benefit rule.

Lump-sum distribution: You take a lump-sum distribution when you withdraw some or all of the value of your 401(k) or other tax-deferred account at one time. By taking a lump sum, you end the tax-deferred status of that asset. You owe income tax on the full value of the distribution at your standard income tax rate. The only exception is if you were born before 1936, in which case you may be able to use ten-year forward averaging to figure the tax you owe.

Management fee: A management fee is the amount an investment company or manager charges to handle the investments you make. For example, if you invest in four different mutual funds offered through your 401(k), you'll pay a management fee, usually figured as a percentage of each account's value, to the company that sponsors the funds.

Each individual fund has its own fee, reflecting the level of management that's required. Generally, index funds cost the least and international equity funds cost the most, though fees differ significantly from one fund company to another.

Matching contribution: A matching contribution is money your employer adds to your 401(k) account. It's usually a percentage of the amount you contribute. The matching amount and any earnings are tax deferred until you withdraw them from your account. Employers are not required to match contributions, but may do so if they wish. Employers also determine, within federal guidelines, how long you have to work for the company in order to be fully vested in the matching contributions.

Minimum distribution incidental benefit (MDIB): If your 401(k) beneficiary is more than ten years younger than you are and isn't your spouse, you must figure your joint life expectancy using the minimum distribution incidental benefit rule. The rule assumes there is a maximum ten-year age difference between you and the beneficiary, even if the actual difference between your ages is much greater.

The reason for the rule is to prevent you from stretching out your required distributions for 30 or 40 years or longer, which also stretches out the income tax you owe on the amounts you withdraw. After your death, however, your age and your beneficiary's actual age determines life expectancy for future distributions.

The MDIB rule doesn't apply if you name your spouse as beneficiary. You may use your spouse's actual age to determine your joint life expectancy.

Minimum required distribution (MRD): A minimum required distribution is the smallest amount you can take each year from your 401(k), traditional IRA, or other retirement savings plan once you've reached the mandatory age for making withdrawals. If you take less than the required minimum, you owe a 50% penalty on the amount you should have taken.

You calculate your MRD by dividing your account balance at the end of your plan's fiscal year—usually but not always December 31—by your life expectancy or the joint life expectancy of you and your beneficiary.

Nondiscrimination rule: All 401(k) plans must follow nondiscrimination rules, which mean, among other things, that highly paid employees aren't treated better than other employees.

Pension maximization: Pension maximization is a strategy that involves selecting a single life annuity for income paid from your plan, and then using some of your annuity income to buy a life insurance policy on your life. At your death, the annuity income ends and the life insurance death benefit is available to provide income for your surviving spouse.

While you receive more income from a single life annuity than from a joint and survivor annuity, there may be potential drawbacks of pension max, as it is sometimes called. These include the cost of insurance, sales charges, and an increased risk of your spouse's running out of income.

Plan administrator: Your 401(k) plan administrator is the person your employer assigns to manage the company's retirement savings plan. The administrator works with the plan provider to ensure that the plan meets government regulations and that you and other employees have the information you need to enroll, select, and change investments in the plan, apply for a loan if the plan allows loans, and request distributions.

Plan provider: A 401(k) plan provider is the mutual fund company, insurance company, brokerage firm, or other financial services company that creates the plan your employer selects.

Plan sponsor: A 401(k) plan sponsor is an employer who offers a plan to a company's employees. The sponsor is responsible for choosing the plan, the plan provider, and the plan administrator, and for deciding which investments will be offered through the plan.

Power of attorney: A power of attorney is a written document that gives someone the authority to act for you or on your behalf. For example, you may give someone a limited power of attorney to handle your day-to-day finances. Or you may give a person or organization, such as a trust company or IRA custodian, a durable power of attorney to make all decisions for you if you are unable or unavailable to make them. These decisions include choosing a beneficiary for your 401(k), selecting a method of calculating life expectancy, and handling required minimum distributions.

A power of attorney must be notarized by a notary public to be legal. It's usually a good idea to consult an attorney to be sure the document you're signing will give the person you're designating the necessary authority to act for you.

Pretax contribution: A pretax contribution is money that you agree to have subtracted from your salary and put into a retirement savings plan or other employer sponsored benefit plan. Your taxable earnings are reduced by the amount of your contribution, which reduces the income tax you owe in the year you make the contribution.

Some pretax contributions, including those you put into your 401(k), are taxed when you withdraw the amount from your plan. Other contributions, such as money you put into a flexible spending plan, are never taxed.

Private letter ruling: A private letter ruling explains a position the Internal Revenue Service (IRS) has taken on a specific issue or action that affects the amount of income tax a taxpayer owes. For example, one letter ruling from 1998 agreed that IRA distributions made to a charitable organization at the participant's death are tax exempt.

While these rulings are not the law, and there's no guarantee that they won't be overturned by new IRS opinions, they can provide guidance in handling taxable distributions from your 401(k) or IRA.

Qualified plan: A qualified plan, such as a 401(k), is a retirement savings plan that's entitled to certain tax benefits for the plan sponsor, provided the plan complies with the regulations of the US tax code section 401. Your employer can sponsor a qualified plan, or you can create one for yourself if you're self-employed.

Some other retirement savings plans share certain features with qualified plans, including tax-deferred earnings and early withdrawal penalties, but aren't considered qualified plans. These include 403(b) plans, and individual retirement accounts (IRAs).

Recalculation: Recalculation is one method of figuring life expectancy. To recalculate, you look up your age in the Internal Revenue Service (IRS) actuarial tables each year to find the life expectancy for that age. If you're married, some 401(k) plans and traditional IRAs automatically recalculate your life expectancy each year to determine your minimum required distribution. You may be able to select other methods for calculating life expectancy, including either the term certain or hybrid method.

Required beginning date (RBD): Your required beginning date is the date by which you must take your first minimum required distribution from retirement savings plans that require distributions. For an individual retirement account (IRA), it's April 1 following the year you turn 70½. For a 401(k), it's either April 1 following the year you turn 70½ or April 1 following the year you retire, unless you own 5% or more of the company sponsoring the plan. If that's the case, the deadline is April 1 after you turn 70½.

Retitled individual retirement account (Retitled IRA): When your beneficiary inherits your traditional or rollover IRA at your death, the account may be retitled. In cases where your beneficiary is your spouse, the account can be transferred to your spouse and registered in your spouse's name. But if your beneficiary is anyone but your spouse, the account must be retitled in your name as the deceased owner for the benefit of the beneficiary. It may not be retitled in the name of your beneficiary.

Rollover individual retirement account (Rollover IRA): You may open a rollover IRA—sometimes called an IRA rollover—with money from an existing tax-deferred account such as another IRA, a 401(k), or a 403(b). You can roll over any amount into the new account, either by arranging a direct transfer from the existing account to the new account, or by moving the money from one account to the other yourself.

If you handle the rollover yourself, 20% of the value of the account you're leaving will be withheld for income taxes. You must also deposit the full amount, including the 20% that's been withheld, into the rollover IRA within 60 days to keep the money tax deferred. That means you'll have to replace the amount that's been withheld for taxes with money from another source.

Salary reduction plan: Employer sponsored retirement savings plans to which you contribute a percentage of your pretax income are sometimes described as salary reduction plans. The salary you don't take home is invested in a tax-deferred account. Rather than being taxed at your current income tax rate, this money will be taxed at the rate you'll be paying when you actually withdraw your contribution and any earnings it has produced.

Tax-deferred account: When you invest through a tax-deferred account, you postpone income tax on any earnings your investments may produce until you withdraw from the account. Tax-deferred accounts are able to compound at a faster rate than accounts from which you withdraw money to pay tax.

The only drawback to a tax-deferred account is that you may have to pay a 10% penalty on any withdrawals you make before you turn 59½, a rule designed to encourage you to save the money for retirement.

Tax-exempt investment: With a tax-exempt investment, there is no income tax due on any interest or dividends the investment produces. A Roth IRA is a tax-exempt investment. So are municipal bonds, which are free of federal income tax and sometimes state and local income tax.

However, you may owe capital gains tax if you sell a tax-exempt municipal bond for more than you paid for it, or if you receive more than par value from the issuer when the bond is redeemed. In addition, some municipal bond income may be subject to the alternative minimum tax (AMT). But withdrawals from a Roth IRA are never taxed if you're older than 59½ and your account has been open at least five years.

Term certain: Term certain is a method of calculating life expectancy. When you use the term certain method, you find your life expectancy just once, for the year in which you turn 70½. You divide your account balance by that number to find your minimum required distribution for the first year you must take money from your account. Each following year you subtract a "1" from the life expectancy you used the year before, and then use the new number in calculating your next minimum required distribution.

Term certain can also be a fixed period of time, typically a specific number of years. For example, if you choose a 15-year term certain for receiving annuity income, the income will be paid each year for 15 years, either to you if you're alive or to your beneficiary if you die during the term. At the end of the fifteenth year, the payments end.

Transfer: In a transfer, a 401(k) or IRA custodian or trustee moves the assets in your existing account directly to the custodian or trustee of your new account. With a transfer, you don't risk failing to deposit the full amount of your withdrawal within the 60-day deadline for rollovers. And, in the case of a transfer from a 401(k) or similar retirement savings plan, nothing is withheld for income taxes. In contrast, if you handle the rollover yourself, your employer must withhold 20% of the account value.

Trustee: A trustee is a person or institution appointed to manage assets for someone else's benefit. For example, a trustee may be responsible for money you have transferred to a trust, or money in certain retirement accounts. Trustees are entitled to collect a fee for their work, often a percentage of the value of the amount in trust. In turn, they are responsible for managing the assets in the best interests of the beneficiary of the trust.

Valuation: Valuation means determining the dollar value of your 401(k) plan or IRA account as of a specific date. When you are taking minimum required distributions from your 401(k) or IRA, the amount you must take is determined by the final valuation of your account for the plan's previous fiscal year, divided by your life expectancy.

Vesting: Vesting is the process of gaining full right to the contributions your employer has made to a retirement plan on your behalf. If you leave before you're fully vested, you forfeit all or part of those amounts. But when you've been on the job for the number of years required by your plan, you gain a nonforfeitable, or vested, right to the contributions.

Withdrawal: In regard to retirement savings plans, a withdrawal is money you take out of your 401(k), IRA, or other plan. If you withdraw before you turn 59½, you may owe a 10% early withdrawal penalty plus any income tax that's due on the amount. In everyday usage, the term withdrawal is used interchangeably with distribution to describe money you take from your tax-deferred accounts.

INDEX

INDEX

INDEX